CRIMES & CAPERS
of the
NORTHWEST

Heather Vale Goss

© 2010 by Folklore Publishing
First printed in 2010 10 9 8 7 6 5 4 3 2 1
Printed in Canada

The Publisher: Folklore Publishing
Website: www.folklorepublishing.com

Library and Archives Canada Cataloguing in Publication

Vale Goss, Heather, 1968–
    Crimes and capers of the Northwest / Heather Vale Goss.

Includes bibliographical references.

ISBN 978-1-926677-52-1

    1. Criminals—Northwest, Pacific—Biography. 2. Crime—Northwest, Pacific—History. I. Title.

HV6805.V36 2010   364.1092'2795   C2009-906812-5

Project Director: Faye Boer
Project Editor: Jordan Allan
Production: Kamila Kwiatkowska; Lisa Morley
Cover Image: © Jean Schweitzer / iStockphoto.com

We acknowledge the support of the Alberta Foundation for the Arts for our publishing program.
We acknowledge the financial support of the Government of Canada through the Book Publishing Industry Development Program (BPIDP) for our publishing activities.

Canadian   Patrimoine
Heritage   canadien

PC: 5

Table of Contents

Dedication

This book is dedicated to my fellow investigator into the human mind and behavior, and my partner in the journey of life, Barry Goss, who inspires and motivates me. Also to our son, Konan Goss, who's full of curiosity at the way the world works and is the light of our lives.

Acknowledgements

To Barry, thank you for your love, support and encouragement. To Konan, thank you for showing me how to look at the world with wide-eyed fascination once again.

To my dad, Elwood, long-time historian, archivist and author, thanks for giving me the genes of research and writing, and teaching me that history can be fun. To my mom, Dee, thanks for helping to foster my creativity and leading by example.

My gratitude to the researchers, reporters and authors who went before me, poring over official documents, historical papers and police files to compose the articles, news reports and books that served as the backbone to my research. My job was much easier thanks to your hard work, and you're all mentioned in the back of this book, whether you inspired me to write a few words or a few pages. To Gary C. King, Gregg Olsen and David Lohr, special thanks for helping further that research by pointing me in the right direction, and for answering my questions about true crime.

Finally, thank you to Folklore Publishing for giving me the opportunity to tackle this unique project. I often write about successes in life, so this is like the yin to that yang, and in many ways just as fascinating.

❧✦☙

Introduction

History is indeed little more than the register of the crimes, follies and misfortunes of mankind.

—Edward Gibbon (1737–94), English historian and
Member of Parliament

This book may be about true crimes, but it isn't necessarily a typical true crime book. Yes, there are a few stories in here about serial killers, but there are also stories about quirky criminals and their intriguing capers. There are stories in which the victims unfortunately died, but others where they fought back or where no one was hurt. There are stories in which the main character seems to show no remorse but others in which the individual is tortured by his or her own wrongdoings. Some of the cases are more current and took place during our lifetimes, while others happened a century or more ago.

I could have included many more stories about the sensational and horrific crimes that have taken place in the Pacific Northwest, but I didn't want to sensationalize crimes, to horrify people who read about them or to cause pain to any of the victims. I'm a journalist, but I've never been an ambulance chaser or crime-beat reporter. Although I worked with some of them during my time in radio news, I was turned off by their desire to discuss the gory details of gruesome, senseless crimes.

Then again, while I've chosen not to follow that route, I do understand how digging into the details could be of value when handled responsibly. Just as crimes are often sensationalized, they're also often glamorized. As true crime writer Gary C. King explained to me, "I feel the need to make a best-effort attempt to show what happened from a victim's perspective in any given case, depicting the how and why of a case through the eyes of the investigators. This often involves showing fully the unpleasant details of a crime, which victims' families have told me they appreciate because it portrays the killer in a more accurate, and hence less glamorous, manner to the reading public."

In this book, I hope to have struck a balance between the two, neither sensationalizing nor glamorizing these true-life stories. And while the length and format of this book also made it necessary to forgo a lot of the facts, I've focused on what I feel are the most important details to tell the story properly. For some readers, this book may be just the beginning of a journey into some of these crimes and capers. You're welcome to start with my sources listed in the back of the book, if that's the case for you.

My main motivation in writing this book stems from my fascination with the way the human mind works, both in cases where it works extremely well, as in the genius mind, and also where it appears "broken," as in the criminal mind. What causes someone to turn out "bad" instead of "good," where "good" is defined as displaying normal, common human decency? Is it the parenting he received? The environment she grew up in? One pivotal moment in his life? Typical patterns, experiences and indicators she embodied? Or regular human emotions and motivators—the Seven Deadly Sins, such as greed and envy—gone ballistic?

Or is "bad" really just a complementary extension of "good"—the yin to the yang, the down to the up, the dark to the light—that exist on both sides of the same coin and can't live without each other? We are all guilty of thinking of ourselves first; do criminals just take it one step too far, thinking only of themselves? While most of us have the tendency to get angry sometimes, or to go after what we want, we temper that desire with respect for other people. Are criminals simply so consumed with their own egos that fellow humans have just become stumbling blocks on what they perceive as their road to success?

This is my first time tackling the true crime genre; usually I write about things that inspire and help people to become more successful in one or more of the important areas of life, such as personal development, entrepreneurship, parenting and health. But to truly know the value of a coin—in this case, the human mind—we have to examine both sides of it, taking the "good" with the "bad." I know many people who do their best to hide from the negatives in life—refusing to watch the news, cocooning themselves away and trying to be upbeat all the time—but instead of being fulfilled, they end up deluding themselves, living in denial and fear of what they're hiding from. They don't understand that the only way to overcome your fears is to face them head on.

As personal development author Vernon Howard wrote in *50 Ways to See Thru People,* "Some students of human nature are reluctant about exposing falseness and weakness in others. They think they should not see so much badness. The opposite is right. You should and must know all about hurtful human behavior, for only exposure of the wrong can invite the right. The real peril is to not see things as they are, for delusion is dangerous to the deluded. Believing that a shark is a dolphin is both foolish and unnecessary. When a wise man sees a shark, he knows it is a shark. Since when is it wrong to see right?"

Along those same lines, Gary Ryan Blair, a goal-setting expert that my husband and I once interviewed together, told us quite plainly, "Behavior doesn't lie." People sabotage themselves daily by saying they want something but behaving in a way that makes it impossible. For example, someone says that he wants to lose weight but eats high-fat junk food as he sits on the couch. A person may say she wants to make more money but doesn't look for opportunities to do so. Someone says he wants to follow a passion but puts it on the back burner to pursue "someday."

Criminals also sabotage themselves with their behavior. They rob a bank to achieve financial freedom, but end up in prison—anything but free. They wish for missing love or acceptance, but then go out and torture, rape or kill— actions that are anything but loving or accepting.

So in the end, maybe criminals aren't all that different from the rest of us; they're just amplified to the extreme. They're more intense, more mixed up, more misguided and more willing to sabotage themselves, and others, in the long term if it means gratification in the short term. And they almost always seem to have the belief that it's impossible to get what they want except at somebody else's expense.

This book may ask more questions than it answers in these regards, but I'd like to think it answers most of the questions about what happened during the crimes and capers in question. We may never know all the "whys" of the crimes, but we can know the "who, what, where, when and how" of each one. And afterwards, we can contemplate the "whys," to try to understand the core of human nature and to recognize the warning signs so we can possibly prevent such episodes from happening again. Because even when violence or crime seems senseless, there's nothing that says we can't try to make some sense of it. If it's true that "everything happens for a reason," why not try to uncover that reason? And if it's not true, why not try to discover what did make it happen? After all, nobody can argue with the fact that every action has a motive, whether or not the motive is logical or sane.

To further that intention, I will sometimes ask rhetorical questions that allow us to consider why a criminal did what he or she did, looking at the possible mindsets, rationalizations, triggers and motivations for what went on. We might not like what we see, or even come close to truly understanding it; after all, we may be dealing with minds that are sick, twisted or so far into their fantasy lives that there's not much rational thinking left. And while there may be certain patterns that emerge, every person is different and some may not have even known why they were doing what they did. But we do have a right to ask.

Gary C. King said to me, "I am drawn to true crime because I am fascinated with the criminal mind, and what makes certain types of people tick and do what they do. It is also the aftermath of the crime and how it has affected peoples' lives that stirs my emotions and motivates me to write about a particular case. Truth is very much stranger than fiction."

True crime writer Gregg Olsen added, "For writers and readers, true crime allows us a glimpse into the unthinkable and tragic. We're all looking for understanding…the best of true crime is the kind that seeks to illuminate, rather than merely entertain."

David Lohr, a true crime writer and former crime investigator for the Discovery Channel, has a slightly different stance. He told me, "For me, true crime was always about trying to understand why criminals do what they do…at least it was until a few years ago, when I decided that trying to understand them was a waste of time. They are, in my opinion, beyond the understanding of anyone who is not exactly like them. I mean, seriously, how do you attempt to understand someone who is capable of raping and murdering a child or cold-bloodedly torturing an elderly person? You can't, unless you are just as sick as they are, and the majority of us who care aren't."

But I still want to try, even if it may be naïve. I feel like that little kid who always asks, "But why?" Knowing "why" can provide comfort and can provide clues to stop it from happening again.

As Nancy Gabbert—mother of 17-year-old Green River Killer victim Sandra Gabbert—once said, "Fifty-four years ago, Gary Ridgway was a darling, adorable, lovable little baby. He's not some monster that dropped down on us from another planet…There's a lot we need to learn." And I'd like to invite you on that journey of learning. The same can be said of every criminal, every victim and every character in these stories—we all started out perfect and innocent. Along the way, we all change to varying degrees.

While all the main elements of all these stories are completely factual, I've taken some artistic license, occasionally adding feelings and thoughts that I think the players may have had, and some dialogue that may or may not have occurred. Each chapter starts with a pivotal moment, interaction or conversation in the case, and then fills you in on what led to that point and what happened afterwards. This is meant to enhance the investigation, entertain you, make you feel as if you're watching the tale unfold, move the story along and avoid making this book seem like a newspaper report. Yes, I may be a journalist, but I was a creative writer first; the result is creative non-fiction. I hope these stories are as interesting, illuminating and enjoyable for you to read as they were for me to put together for you.

CHAPTER ONE

Bill Miner
The Gentleman Bandit
(1847–1913)

Don't steal. The government hates competition.

—Anonymous

"Dammit," he yelled as he fumbled nervously with the lit sticks of dynamite. This was Bill Miner's first ever train robbery, but it wasn't going well. He had successfully committed many stagecoach robberies before—and spent half his life in prison as a result—so why should a train robbery be so different?

A famous robber named John Chapman had laid out the template for successfully robbing trains over 30 years ago, before Miner's last stint in San Quentin State Prison, which had lasted nearly two decades. The Chapman method of robbing trains was simple: he hopped on a train in the middle of nowhere when it slowed down or stopped. Then he climbed over the coal car into the locomotive, pulled a gun on the engineer and forced him to stop the train.

Since gold was always carried in the express car safe, and the express and baggage cars were always right behind the engine, Chapman would unhook the two cars and make the engineer take them a few miles away, leaving the unwitting passengers behind. Express cars were always locked and guarded with armed attendants, so he would demand that the guards open the door or else watch it blasted open with dynamite.

So here was 55-year-old Bill Miner, on the Oregon Railroad and Navigation Company's Fast Express train to Chicago on September 23, 1903, trying to follow in the footsteps of success. He had two younger accomplices with him: 17-year-old orphan Charles Hoehn from Whatcom, Washington, and 25-year-old Guy Harshman from Portland, Oregon. Miner and Harshman had hidden in the shadows and climbed aboard the train at the Portland freight sheds, then made their move when it reached the way station of Troutdale. Miner had his gun trained on the engineer, Ollie Barrett, and the fireman, H.F. Stevenson, and had forced them to stop the train near Mile Post 21, where Hoehn was waiting with his rifle and two poles that had dynamite tied to the ends.

"No trickery, or your only reward will be death," Harshman told the train crew, who seemed eager enough to comply. Miner made Barrett carry the dynamite as he and Harshman escorted the two trainmen to the baggage car at gunpoint, and Hoehn fired his gun to warn nosy passengers to stay away.

"It's me, Barrett…open the door," Barrett shouted to the express car messenger, Fred Korner. But Korner and his assistant, Solomon Glick, had agreed to only use that particular phrase when a robbery was underway, so they stayed silent.

When nobody opened the baggage car's doors, Miner resorted to the dynamite method. Barrett and Stevenson must have known they were dealing with amateurs, since more experienced train robbers would have dynamited the express car, where all the valuable cargo was located, instead of the baggage car. Their suspicions were confirmed when they saw Miner's obvious nervousness setting the charges, and when they witnessed what happened next—Harshman ran towards the blasted-open baggage doors instead of making the trainmen go first as human shields.

Inside the baggage car, Korner was ready and waiting with his shotgun, and he leaned out and fired towards the men. In the smoke and darkness, he wasn't really sure who he was aiming at and ended up shooting Harshman in the head and engineer Barrett in the shoulder. Both men collapsed as Miner shot back, causing Korner to retreat. When Miner knelt down to check on his partner-in-crime, who had fallen in the ditch beside the tracks, it looked like Harshman was dead.

"Get back in your cab!" Miner shouted in panic at the trainmen, just before he and Hoehn escaped, empty-handed, down the bank of the nearby Columbia River. Miner felt like a complete failure. He was used to pulling off successful robberies and had been doing so since he was a teenager.

There's some debate over when Miner was born—his birth date has been variously recorded as 1842, 1843, 1846 or 1847, with most accounts settling on 1847—and where—some say Michigan, while others say Kentucky, and American detectives recorded his nationality as Canadian. However, he was almost certainly born Ezra Allen Miner and changed his first name to William at age 18.

Miner attended school until he was 16, receiving additional lessons from his mother and two grandmothers. His mother had been having financial problems since his father died, when Miner was only 10 years old, so she moved the family out west to a mining town near Auburn, California. He briefly joined the Union Army in 1864 during the American Civil War and was assigned to a Sacramento military base. But Miner had always hated discipline, so he deserted four months later, just as he would eventually escape from jail so many times.

He worked in Texas and New Mexico as a cowhand, a gold prospector and a Pony Express rider, but it was from being a regular passenger on express stagecoaches that inspired his next career move. Miner couldn't help but notice the large amount of gold that was being shipped by coach, and knowing where and when it was going, he found it hard to resist the implications of that knowledge. Insofar as temptation enters all our lives, it takes a certain high-risk personality to follow through with it despite the probable consequences.

The first time Miner robbed a Wells Fargo stagecoach, he got away with $75,000. Then he promptly went to jail for the crime, spending three years in San Quentin for the first time. He was released in 1869 and went right back to robbing stagecoaches.

Eventually, people started calling Bill Miner the "North American Robin Hood." And while it may be true that he only robbed the rich—people that he figured could "afford to lose it"—he didn't really distribute the wealth back to the poor, unless you count him and his gangs as "poor."

Miner was the most polite bandit people had ever come across. He would not only apologize to the passengers, but would tell the driver, after robbing him, to be careful on the roads. He always carried a gun but rarely used it.

After two years of successful holdups, Miner was arrested again and found himself back in San Quentin with a 10-year sentence. A few months later, he was tried for another holdup and sentenced to an additional 12 years. Never one to do as he was told, Miner escaped in 1874, but was free for only a couple of hours before being thrown back in the slammer.

This time, however, he was labeled as troublesome. Miner was beaten by the guards in the prison yard in front of the other prisoners and then locked in the dark and dismal dungeon, where his cell was nothing more than a hole cut into the side of a damp stone tunnel. If anyone in the dungeon caused problems, the guards would quiet the prisoner down by splashing a solution of heated limestone and water, known as "quicklime," onto his cell floor, which caused a chemical reaction that gave off toxic fumes.

When Miner was finally allowed to leave the dungeon and go back to his regular cell, he was forced to wear a weighted shackle on his leg called the Oregon Boot, which was invented by a warden at the Oregon State Penitentiary. It was designed to throw off the prisoner's balance and to make escape more difficult.

After serving nine years of his sentence, Miner was released in 1880. Now 33 years old, he had spent nearly all of his adult life locked up and had an overwhelming desire to live life to its fullest. He also decided to try out a new name to go with his new freedom: William A. Morgan.

Miner worked his way towards Colorado, where he joined forces with a noted Rocky Mountain bandit named Billy Leroy. Together they robbed a stagecoach near Del Norte, making off with $3600 in coins and gold dust.

"Hands up!" Miner yelled at the driver, pointing his gun at him. Real and fictional robbers would use this phrase for years to come, but Miner is credited with being the first to say it. Just a few minutes later, the robbery was finished. "Sorry about that," Miner said to the passengers. "Cost you a 10-minute delay." Then he turned to the driver and said, "You take care now, the roads are pretty treacherous around here."

After the holdup, Miner and Leroy separated to avoid being caught. While Miner headed north, Leroy brazenly pulled another stagecoach robbery and ended up being hanged by an enraged lynch mob of local citizens.

After spending some time in Michigan and wooing a young woman from a well-off family by claiming to be a rich heir himself, Miner headed back to Colorado. He partnered with an old buddy, Stanton T. Jones, and again held up the Del Norte stagecoach, but this time the duo didn't get much. Still, Miner was his usual courteous self. "Sorry for the intrusion," he said. "You have a good night, now!"

Lew Armstrong was the local sheriff of Del Norte, Colorado, and he was quite good at catching robbers. As Miner and Jones galloped off on a couple of stolen horses, a settler looking for some reward money saw them crossing a bridge and tipped off Sheriff Armstrong, who quickly captured the bandits.

Miner, though, was still a master of escape. That night, while a wagon driver was watching over the prisoners, Miner pulled out a hidden gun that the sheriff hadn't found. "You untie us, right now!" he ordered the scared driver. Armstrong, hearing the commotion, came out with his rifle, but Miner fired back—one of the few times he pulled his trigger. Even in the dark, he had good aim, and his shots injured Armstrong and his men but didn't kill them.

Miner and Jones escaped into the night, stole a couple more horses and headed for Arizona. They ultimately worked their way towards California, but along the way, they kept robbing stagecoaches.

"Hands up!" the stagecoach drivers would hear each time. Then Miner would take whatever he could from the passengers—gold, wallets, jewelry and other valuables—and follow it up with a polite apology and a "Good night!"

Miner sported a couple of unique tattoos—a ballet dancer on his right arm and a heart and dagger on his left—that passengers sometimes noticed during these holdups. These tattoos had also been noted by San Quentin officials and passed on to the Pinkerton Detective Agency, which was the premier agency for investigating stagecoach and train robberies in those days. For years, the Pinkertons had been adding to Bill Miner's file, and by now it was getting quite thick. So when reports of a polite robber with a ballet dancer tattoo came in, they knew exactly who was responsible. Following the string of robberies, they figured, correctly, that Miner was headed to California.

However, when Miner finally reached the California border, he slipped in quietly and easily, since the Pinkerton Agency thought he was still somewhere in Arizona or Utah. Miner was now going by the name William Anderson and hid out in a small mining community named Chinese Camp while he recovered from a severe bout of the flu. "I'm not going this way," he said to those around him. "I'll be better soon, you'll see!" Sure enough, his strong will to survive saved him just when it looked like he might not make it.

While at the mining camp, he met up with some fellow thieves who liked his never-say-die attitude: namely, Jim Connor, Bill Miller and James Crum. Miner convinced them to help him rob Wells Fargo's Sonora-Milton stagecoach, which regularly carried gold from the Angels Camp mines.

At this point, Miner became a bit too confident. Maybe it was his renewed health, or maybe it was the same thing that causes many men to act foolishly—a woman. While checking out the coach schedule, the men attended a dance at Angels Camp, and Miner became smitten with a girl who was singing there. He told her he was heading to San Francisco but would return for her, and that he would send her some sheet music in the meantime.

The next day, Miner and his men held up the stagecoach for $3250 in gold coins and $500 in gold dust from one of the passengers. "Sorry for the delay," Miner said, before sending the coach on its way. Of course, the Pinkerton detectives quickly heard about the robbery and sent their chief investigator for Wells Fargo, Detective Aull, to check it out. Aull found out that Miner had been at the dance and had a little chat with the singer. Two weeks later, when Miner sent her some sheet music as promised, she reported him and the hunt was on.

As Miner and Crum headed back to the mining camp to see the girl, they realized that they were being tailed. They decided to take a detour to Bill Miller's farm, but Aull was coincidentally headed there, too, because Miller had just been identified as one of the robbers. Crum was caught at the farm, and Miller was picked up after he and Miner had a brief run-in with Aull, who claimed to be a wayward duck hunter looking for his pals. Miner managed to escape, but

Aull tracked him down a short time later and persuaded him to surrender.

Aull took the three men to Sacramento, where they were interrogated separately. Miner and Miller refused to spill the beans, but Crum sang like a jailbird so he wouldn't have to be one for long and gave up both his partners. In December 1881, Miner was convicted once again of stagecoach robbery and given the maximum sentence of 25 years, thanks in part to his huge file at the Pinkerton agency.

It's hard to tell what might have been going through Miner's mind when he headed back to San Quentin. The guards watched him closely because of his previous reputation as a troublemaker, but for over four years, he was on his best behavior and worked hard in the prison jute mill. That may have been just so they'd let their guard down, literally, because at that point, Miner escaped again. But as before, he was only out for a few hours before being brought back to the slammer. His little adventure cost him dearly, erasing his entire good behavior record and causing him to spend the next few years in the dungeon.

Finally, in June 1902, after serving nearly 20 years in prison, Miner was free once more. He took on a new moniker, Bill Morgan, and headed to his sister's house in Whatcom, Washington, to figure out what he was going to do with what was left of his life. The world had completely changed in those 20 years he was behind bars, especially for stagecoach robbers. Newspapers and telegraphs helped better track criminals, the Pinkerton Detective Agency now had photos on file to help eyewitnesses identify suspects, and the stagecoaches were being phased out, partly thanks to robbers like Miner. Gold mine managers didn't like how easy it was for bandits to track their gold shipments, rob the coaches and ride off into the sunset, so they now used trains to ship their valuable bullion.

Robbing trains turned out to be a puzzle that bandits didn't figure out until John Chapman came along with his successful method. At Miner's age, though, the Chapman method wasn't the easiest caper to pull off. Many crooks in Miner's position would have retired, but Miner was more persistent than most. After all, at San Quentin, he had been beaten, forced to breathe caustic lime fumes and had spent years in total blackness. Rather than being broken down by the torture, he had become more hardened and his senses had become sharper.

He also knew how to manipulate people weaker than himself, so it was easy to convince novice accomplices like Charles Hoehn and Guy Harshman to help him out. Harshman had already spent some time in San Quentin, which is where he met Miner, but Hoehn's only previous criminal experience had been a bit of petty theft.

And that brings us back to Miner's unsuccessful robbery of the Oregon Railroad and Navigation Company train. It was actually his second failure in Oregon—the first time, four days earlier on September 19, the train had thundered past Miner and Harshman without slowing down as they expected because they had misread the stop signals. At least this time, they had made it on board.

After Miner and Hoehn took off, leaving Harshman for dead, the train crew reported the attempted robbery to the Multnomah County Sheriff's Department in Portland, as well as to the Pinkerton Detective Agency. Sheriff William Storey and Pinkerton Portland Superintendent Captain

James Nevins headed to the scene of the crime and discovered Harshman in the ditch, still clinging to life but partially paralyzed.

After Harshman miraculously recovered, he gave a fake name and refused to tell police anything. Several false leads and incorrect arrests later, investigators finally figured out Harshman's real identity and discovered that he had served time in both Washington and California for counterfeiting. Since there was no point in lying anymore, he told Sheriff Storey that his gang had consisted of four other people, including Bill Morgan and his nephew, Charles Morgan, who lived in Whatcom.

The Pinkerton detectives had already been given a lead about Charles, so Storey went to Whatcom and ferreted him out. Based on Harshman's descriptions of Bill Morgan, though, Storey figured he was really looking for Bill Miner and went directly to Miner's sister's home, where Miner had taken Harshman's bloody overcoat. But Miner, once again, had already escaped…and this time, he couldn't be found. While Harshman and Hoehn were sentenced to prison time, Miner headed to Canada.

In Princeton, British Columbia, Miner made a new life for himself masquerading as a Texan named George W. Edwards. He stayed with a local family for the winter, acting like a perfect gentleman and often giving the kids quarters as they headed off to school. After that, Miner moved in with a man named Jack Budd who lived nearby, and who, some say, was actually Miner's brother. Another local man, William "Shorty" Dunn, soon became Miner's new friend and next partner-in-crime. Even though the men were away from home when the next train robbery happened, nobody ever suspected this kindly southern gentleman of being involved.

It was September 10, 1904, almost a year after Miner's first botched train robbery. The Canadian Pacific's Transcontinental Express No. 1 was making its way slowly through a thick fog in Mission Junction, British Columbia, on its way to Vancouver.

Engineer Nathaniel J. Scott turned when he felt a hand on his shoulder and heard the words, "Hands up!" He found himself face to face with a masked and armed Miner, who had two more masked men behind him—Shorty Dunn and Jake Terry, a convict from Washington who Miner had met in San Quentin.

Terry used to work as a railroad engineer, so he knew his way around trains. He had met up with the other two robbers near the Canada-Washington border, and all three had climbed aboard the train when it went by. As the train picked up speed, they climbed over the other cars and sneaked into the engine room.

"Stop the train at the Silverdale crossing," Miner ordered Scott as Terry trained his rifle on him. Scott knew he had no other choice and did as he was told. Then Miner told the train's fireman, Harry Freeman, to accompany him to the express car to uncouple the train. While they did this, the crew began to panic. The brakeman, Bill Abbott, figured something was up and soon found himself staring down the barrel of Terry's gun. He retreated back into his car as ordered but told the passengers that a robbery was taking place. The conductor fainted, and the porter panicked and started yelling, "The engineer's been killed!" Abbott escaped and ran five miles along the train track back to

Mission Junction to report the crime, but nobody there believed him.

Throughout the commotion, it would have been easy for Miner to get nervous again, as he had during his first train robbery attempt. However, he kept his cool this time, and his gang followed suit. Once the express car was uncoupled, Miner and Dunn took Freeman back to the engine, where Scott was still alive and being held at gunpoint. "Take us to the church by the Whonock mile post," Miner told him.

Terry stayed with Scott and Freeman while Miner and Dunn went to the express car. The express messenger, Herbert Mitchell, looked out and, finally realizing what was going on, grabbed his gun. "Open the door, or we'll blow it down with dynamite!" Miner shouted to him. Mitchell and another crewmember tried jumping out at the robbers to surprise them, but Miner and Dunn captured them and took Mitchell's gun. Then they forced him to open the safe, where they found $6000 worth of gold dust and $1000 cash. Miner also grabbed some parcels and registered mail, which contained $50,000 in U.S. bonds and $200,000 in Australian securities.

Still, Miner was expecting something more. He kept searching and finally asked Mitchell, "Where's the chest of gold that's supposed to be on this train?" Mitchell told him that the $62,000 worth of bullion that Miner was referring to had been transferred to another train because of a last-minute delay.

The entire holdup had taken only half an hour, and even without the gold, the bandits knew they were done. Miner threw away the fireman's coal shovel so they'd have to fuel the engine by hand and told Scott, "Careful backing up.

You've got no rear lights on the express car." Then he smiled, and said, "Good night, boys! Sorry to have troubled you," before vanishing into the night.

This being Canada's very first train robbery, the authorities didn't know what to do. British Columbia's provincial police force called on the Pinkerton Detective Agency for assistance, and Superintendent James E. Dye, the agency's head in Seattle, was more than happy to help. He was still investigating the attempted Portland robbery from the year before, and he figured the same gang was probably responsible. Since the Canadian train crew said the bandits had American accents, and since the holdup took place just 10 miles from the U.S. border, Dye figured the robbers must have headed into Washington.

Unfortunately, all his leads went nowhere. First, the Pinkertons mistakenly arrested a detective working on another case because they saw him loitering around Sumas, Washington, just south of Mission Junction. Then they ambushed three men in a cabin near Ferndale, who turned out to be innocent homesteaders who had definitely been in Seattle on the night of the robbery.

Meanwhile, an independent tracker found some footprints that led into Canada, the opposite direction from where Dye had his men searching, but the BC police ignored him. The Canadian Pacific Railway had offered a $5000 reward, which was matched by the Canadian government, and to boot, the British Columbia provincial government added a bonus of $500 per robber to anyone who could capture them. But nobody was ever able to claim the reward money.

In the end, all Dye could do was make a note on Bill Miner's file. He knew that Miner was the only robber who was polite enough to fit the leader's description in both the Oregon and Canadian holdups; he just didn't know where to look for him.

Since Miner was the main suspect, he and Terry decided to split up. Terry headed back to Washington, and Miner and Dunn returned to Budd's ranch in Princeton, telling neighbors they had been out on a hunting trip. That was partially true—they just didn't mention they'd been hunting for gold rather than bears.

Miner and Dunn took another one of those trips in October 1905, around the same time of a Great Northern train robbery at the Raymond brickyard near Seattle, Washington. Although it's never been proven, the robbery has always been attributed to Miner and Terry, with Dunn orchestrating the getaway.

Before the robbery, the crooks cut the phone lines in the area and drove their stolen getaway buggy to a secluded spot north of Ballard. On October 2, Miner waited with the buggy while Terry walked a few miles south to meet the train, which was heading north out of Seattle that evening. Terry jumped aboard as the train passed, then crawled along the roof, over the coal car and into the engine, surprising engineer Caulder and fireman Julette.

"Keep going," Terry ordered them, pointing a pearl-handled revolver their way, "until you see a campfire." When they got to the appointed spot, they stopped the train and Miner came aboard. All four bandits then headed to the express car, where messenger Anderson was told to step away, and Julette was forced to blow open the safe.

The first safe didn't have any money inside, but there was a second one. It took two tries to blast it open, but the robbers got some gold bars and other loot for their troubles and then took off on their horses to where they had hidden the getaway buggy. Since they were in a hurry, they didn't bother untying the hitching strap but cut it instead.

Railroad detective M.E. Ryan called the police as soon as the bandits were out of sight, and Police Chief Bennett, as well as another railroad detective named M.J. Webb, arrived around midnight to investigate. Bennett found the cut piece of hitching strap and followed the tracks left by the horse and buggy. Nearby, they found a revolver and a letter addressed to someone named Fred Alexander.

Later, the train crew was interviewed, and Caulder and Julette described the robbers. They said a tall one had forced them to stop the train, and his partner had called him Tom; a shorter one called Bill had come aboard later—both seemed to be experienced. Although rumor had it that they made off with over $30,000, Great Northern officials insisted it was actually less than $1000.

The next day, the investigation was joined by Marshall J.T. Harrison from Edmonds. He and detective Webb found an abandoned horse and buggy a few miles north of Bitter Lake, along with some switches, rubber pants and a short, double-breasted overcoat. The horse was worn out and a cut hitching strap hung from its neck; obviously, this had been the robbers' getaway buggy.

Once the story hit the local papers, several witnesses came forward. Two hunters mentioned seeing three men in the area the day of the robbery, and after hearing their descriptions of the men, Marshall Harrison realized that he had seen one of them hanging around Edmonds. A few other people reported that they had seen some suspicious-looking men near Ballard, and a farmer named C.H. Thomas said his son had found a discarded canvas moneybag on their property.

The search continued, with Harrison scouring Seattle and the wharves, and Sherriff Lou Smith checking the areas around Lake Washington and Woodinville, while a deputy was sent to Bothell. Within two days of the robbery, Smith said he was sure the culprits were Miner and Terry and added that both had recently been seen in the area. To help capture the men, the Great Northern Railway Company posted a reward of $5000 for each man.

Terry claimed he was in Bellingham the night of the robbery, but according to witnesses, he had purchased a pearl-handled revolver in Seattle shortly before it happened. Still, the police weren't completely sure, and so far, there wasn't enough hard evidence to prosecute Terry or Miner for the crime.

So Smith kept looking for clues and eventually tracked down Fred Alexander, the intended recipient of the letter they'd found. Alexander had a partner named James L. Short, and a Seattle Hardware Company clerk confirmed that Short had indeed bought a gun from him recently, so Smith arrested Short and charged him with stealing the horse and buggy. That was the only arrest ever associated with the 1905 Great Northern train robbery.

Back in Princeton, Miner continued living peacefully as George W. Edwards, charming the locals with his social skills and his gifts of candy for the kids, not to mention the chocolates and flowers for the adults. Six months after the Great Northern train robbery, a former schoolteacher named Louis Colquhoun started hanging out with Miner, Dunn and Budd. Colquhoun only had one previous run-in with the law and had spent two years in the Walla Walla

Penitentiary for petty theft. But on May 8, 1906, he joined Miner and Dunn for another train-robbing adventure.

The Canadian Pacific Railway's Imperial Limited train was heading west to Vancouver when engineer Callin noticed two men crouched on top of the coal car. "What are you doing?" Callin called out to them.

Miner and Dunn pulled their revolvers on Callin and fireman Radcliffe, and Miner said, "Don't do anything foolish, and you won't be harmed." He then ordered Callin to stop the train west of Ducks, near Kamloops, BC, where Colquhoun joined them with an armload of dynamite.

The robbery seemed to be going according to plan, with Miner, Colquhoun and Dunn following all the prescribed steps, while the crew was cooperating graciously. But while searching through the registered mail and finding only 11 letters, they suddenly realized that they had hijacked the baggage car instead of the express car!

"Dammit!" yelled Miner, jerking his revolver violently and letting his mask slip down so that A.L. McQuarrie, one of the mail clerks, got a good look at him. Pulling his mask back up, Miner muttered, "Guess we left the darned express car back with the rest of the train." They looked through the rest of the baggage, and Miner took some liver pills, but they completely missed several flat packages containing $40,000 in bank notes. Despite another dismal failure, Miner was cheerful when they left the train. "Good night, boys...take care!" he called.

The next day, the BC police picked up the trail of the crooks. Again, a reward of up to $11,500 was offered, and all the local papers printed vivid descriptions of the three men. Constable W.L. Fernie was the top tracker, and it took him

less than a week to find the bandits, who didn't recognize
him as a cop. After calling in some backup from Sergeant J.J.
Wilson and his team of Royal North-West Mounted Police,
the police ambushed the robbers while they were casually
eating their lunch. Oddly, they appeared unconcerned about
the intrusion.

Wilson asked the men who they were and what they were
doing, so Miner introduced himself, "I'm George Edwards.
This is Billy Dunn, and that's Louis Colquhoun. We been
prospecting but haven't had much luck around here, so
we're headed back to Princeton."

Wilson was confused but took a stab anyway, telling the
men that they were under arrest for train robbery.

Miner laughed. "We don't look like train robbers," he
bluffed. But Dunn panicked, yelling, "Look out, boys, it's all
up!" and firing his gun into the air. During the ensuing
shoot-out, Dunn was hit in the leg and the other two sur-
rendered. The police searched the campsite and found more
guns, and one of the sergeants recognized Miner from
a wanted poster. Despite the locals' protests that Miner was
actually George W. Edwards, the police escorted the thieves
to a Kamloops jail.

During the ensuing court trial, the jury couldn't come to
a unanimous decision. The joke of the day was, "Bill Miner's
not so bad. He robs the CPR once every two years, but the
CPR robs us all every day." As a result, a second trial was held,
and all three men were found guilty. Miner and Dunn were
sentenced to life imprisonment at the New Westminster
Penitentiary, while Colquhoun, who had a shorter criminal
record, only received 25 years.

But just as the Canadian police didn't know how to handle a train robbery when Miner pulled their first one, the penitentiary didn't know how to keep an eye on prisoners, since they'd never had a jailbreak. And because Miner had vowed to the Kamloops judge, "No prison can hold me, sir," he wanted to be the first to do that, too.

At first the guards kept a close eye on him, but after a year or so, they had already relaxed their guard. The Deputy Warden's daughter, Katherine Bourke, kept bringing Miner religious literature because he had promised her that he really wanted to reform. She finally convinced her father to ease up on the maximum security and to let Miner work in the prison brickyard with the other inmates.

Miner's feet were in bad shape, but nonetheless he worked cheerfully, carting bricks in a wheelbarrow from the yard to the drying kiln. Because of all his hard work, the guards didn't mind when he stopped to rest against the fence after each load. However, three of his fellow inmates soon figured out that he was slowly digging a hole under the fence every time he stopped there, and they started to help him out. John Clarke, Albert McCluskey and Walter John Woods took turns digging with Miner, and as soon as the watchtower guard disappeared inside for a smoke break, Miner dove through the hole, followed closely by the other three. There was a second wall to get over, but Miner knew about a ladder stored in a nearby tool shed, so it was only a matter of picking a lock before the prisoners were out and racing towards the nearest bushes to hide.

Because the guards had to first round up the rest of the prisoners, it took them a half an hour to start pursuing the escapees. But soon every police force in British Columbia and

Washington was on high alert, and the Pinkerton agency was once again circulating Miner's description to the public.

After a while, people began to question whether the "escape" had ever really happened. It turns out that the hole didn't look big enough for a man to fit through, and it might have just been a red herring to disguise the fact that Miner had actually been "handed out," or allowed to go free. It was also later revealed that Miner had had more freedom in prison than was normal at the time: for example, he was allowed to grow his hair while the others were shaved; he met with his lawyer whenever he liked and talked to visitors without having a prison officer present; and he could reply to letters as often as he wished, whereas the standard limitation was one letter per month.

The speculation was that Miner had made a deal with the CPR to return the $50,000 worth of stolen bonds from the 1904 robbery at Mission Junction—which he had never spent because of the risks involved—in exchange for his freedom. Of course, further speculation claims that Miner kept the bonds even after being let go.

Either way, Miner had disappeared and never went back to Budd's ranch in Princeton. Instead, he headed south, worked in a mine for a while, and then in 1909, held up the Portland Oregon Bank for $12,000. Now using the name George Anderson, he got a job at a sawmill in Pennsylvania, where he met his next accomplice, Charles Hunter. It seems that Miner could never stop plotting his next crime, and he didn't have a problem persuading others to take part. Miner and Hunter headed south, recruiting another sawmill employee, George Handsford, in Virginia. By the end of 1910, the three men were working at a sawmill in Georgia, which was conveniently close to the main Southern Express train line.

In February 1911, they committed Georgia's first train robbery. Reportedly, there was $65,000 in gold on board, but it was stashed in a large safe that didn't blow up after three attempts, so the bandits only made off with the $1000 that was in the smaller safe. Police launched an extensive manhunt and found a smiling Bill Miner hiding out in a deserted cabin, as always claiming he had nothing to do with any so-called robbery. Certainly, the frail and sick-looking old man didn't look to be a criminal, but he was locked up in a country jail anyway. His accomplices were soon rounded up, and they confessed to the crime, so Miner followed suit, hoping to get a lenient sentence—instead, he got another 20 years.

Of course, the Canadians wanted him back in New Westminster Penitentiary, Miner liked the way he was treated up there, and W.M. Pinkerton, the head of the agency, knew that a small jail would never hold Miner, so they all agreed that Miner should head back to British Columbia. But the Georgia police wanted to keep him where he was, and, as a result, the ailing old man managed to escape again—not once, but twice.

However, Miner's last escape found him slogging through a swamp full of poisonous snakes, crippled and half-starved. He ended up stumbling right into the waiting arms of the Georgia police, and he was returned to prison, where he died in the hospital on September 2, 1913. The local paper reported Bill Miner's death as his third and final escape from the Georgia prison, never to be caught again.

CHAPTER TWO

Sarah Johnson
The Rebellious Teen
(1987–)

He reminds me of the man who murdered both his parents, and then when the sentence was about to be pronounced, pleaded for mercy on the grounds that he was an orphan.

—Abraham Lincoln (1809–65), politician and president of the United States

Sarah Johnson sat nonchalantly on the fence of the house she'd been living in for years with her parents. It was a beautiful home in the affluent neighborhood of Bellevue, on the outskirts of Sun Valley, Idaho, and the family that lived in it had been fairly close-knit—the parents were longtime sweethearts Alan and Diane Johnson, and they had two picture-perfect children, 22-year-old Matt and 16-year-old Sarah. But just after Labor Day weekend, on Tuesday, September 2, 2003, Sarah's life had changed completely as she watched her murdered parents carried out of the house in body bags.

And for a teenager whose life was changing so drastically, she seemed strangely—suspiciously—aloof about the whole thing.

Shortly after the bodies were found, family and friends began arriving at the house to offer their condolences to the kids. They were understandably devastated and tried to comfort Matt and Sarah. Most of them started accusing Bruno Santos, Sarah's boyfriend, of the crime; he was an illegal alien from Mexico and was three years older than Sarah. It wasn't a secret that Sarah's parents hadn't approved of their relationship—in fact, even Sarah's friends thought she could do better. They all expected that Santos would be convicted of the murders. Everyone was worried about how Sarah was going to deal with the shock, and they stood ready to offer their support.

However, Sarah seemed distant and cold. She went off on her own, ignoring all the well-wishers and watching the police activity instead. Blaine County Sheriff Walt Femling noticed it, too, and told his team of investigators to make note of it. "Most 16-year-olds would be hiding," he said to them, "not sitting there on the fence, watching their parents come out in body bags. No way!"

In the days that followed, Sarah's friends also noticed that she seemed far too concerned with her hair and nail appointments to actually be grieving. One of her friends, Chante Caudle, said that Sarah had come up to her during volleyball practice and had said, "Chante, find Bruno and tell him that I love him, no matter what happens." Caudle felt a chill come over her, and her heart sank, as she suspected that Sarah may have done the horribly unthinkable—murdered her parents in cold blood. Had she shot her own mother in the head and her own father in the chest? Could such a thing even be possible?

The Wood River High School yearbook for 2003 has a picture of Sarah standing with the rest of her junior varsity volleyball team, and her sophomore class photo depicts her smiling happily. This would be the last class photo she ever posed for.

Bruno Santos was a high school dropout who lived across town in a poor neighborhood. Friends and relatives who witnessed the heated arguments in the Johnson household thought that Sarah's insistence on being with him despite her parents' objections was tearing the family apart. One of Sarah's friends, Syringa Stark, said, "He was a high school dropout, selling drugs, and she was from a nice family. It just didn't seem right."

On the Saturday of that fateful Labor Day weekend, Sarah had gone to visit Santos, and Alan and Diane found out that she was planning to sleep over. When Alan picked his daughter up, he got angry at Santos. "Stay away from my daughter," he said, "or I'll report you to the police for having sex with an underage girl!"

Santos may have also been angry, but he obviously didn't want the police involved, seeing as he was a drug dealer and an illegal immigrant. He backed off and let Sarah go.

"But I love him!" Sarah cried on the way home. "I'm not going to let you do anything to him!"

As it turned out, any thoughts Alan had of involving the authorities were permanently squelched because, by Tuesday morning, he and his wife were dead.

When Femling arrived at the crime scene, he was greeted with the most disturbing sight he had ever seen. In the master bedroom—and even out into the hallway—there was blood everywhere, on the floor, walls and ceiling. The first thing Femling did was close down the entire street, stopping a garbage truck that was in the middle of its rounds. Among the garbage, he found some key pieces of evidence: a bloody bathrobe, a left-handed leather glove and a right-handed latex glove.

Investigators were pretty sure that it would be Santos's DNA that they'd find on the gloves and robe, but, thanks to Sarah's behavior that day and gossip among her relatives about the bitter arguments she'd been having with her parents, they decided to take fingerprints and DNA samples from her, too.

When she was interviewed by the police, Sarah kept insisting that a burglar had broken in and had shot her parents, even when it was pointed out to her that there was absolutely no evidence of somebody trying to break in.

Sarah was sent to Caldwell to stay with her mother's sister, Linda Vavold, and her husband, Jim. But Aunt Linda didn't believe Sarah either, since Sarah's story changed every time the police questioned her.

In the middle of October—six weeks after the gruesome double murder—the forensic lab results came back and proved that the DNA found inside the gloves belonged to Sarah. "There it is!" Femling said to his co-workers. "We've got her!"

The investigators were relieved to have solved the case and were pretty sure they'd finally get a confession, so they interrogated Sarah one more time. "But I didn't do it," Sarah kept insisting. Femling didn't want to make the next move without a proper confession, but he was left with no choice. After 45 minutes of stalemate, he arrested the young woman on two counts of first-degree murder and sent her to the Blaine County Jail.

They say that suicide is a permanent solution to a temporary problem. Sarah Johnson also chose a very drastic permanent solution to her temporary problem—and the whole family suffered for her rash decision. Teenagers often fight with their parents, but what caused an otherwise intelligent girl who seemed to have it all to kill her own parents? Was it a crime of passion? Fear over losing someone she loved? Blind rage? A youthful invincibility, thinking she could get away with anything? Or just plain stupidity?

Sarah was born on January 1, 1987, and had always been a popular, smart and athletic girl. Her dad, Alan, who was part owner of a landscaping business, and mom, Diane, who worked at a medical clinic, had provided well for the family, taking care of whatever Sarah or her brother needed.

Apparently Sarah wasn't very grateful for all of that, because she carefully planned her parents' murder before executing it. At six in the morning, when most kids her age were getting ready for the first day of school, she put her bathrobe on backwards, donned a couple of mismatched gloves, walked into her parents' bedroom with a .264-caliber rifle and shot her sleeping mother in the head. After that, she went into the adjoining bathroom and shot her father in the chest as he came rushing out of the shower to see what was going on. Later, she dumped her gloves and bathrobe in the trash, knowing the garbage truck would be coming around soon to pick it up.

It's very rare for a 16-year-old girl to be charged with murdering both her parents. The act of killing one's own parent, called parricide, is usually committed by boys. In fact, over the previous quarter century, there had only been four cases in the U.S. of parricide committed by girls. As a result, Sarah Marie Johnson, high school junior, suddenly found herself the subject of news headlines across the country.

Worried that Sarah's classmates would be harassed by the media, the Blaine County School District implemented a policy prohibiting reporters from hanging around the Wood River High School campus. Meanwhile, Sarah's schooling was put on hold because the Blaine County Jail, where she was being held in a three-person cell with one other woman, was too small to be able to offer her any kind of educational program.

Some of Sarah's relatives came to visit her in jail, but her brother Matt, who was attending university in Moscow, Idaho, wasn't one of them. He wasn't about to forgive his sister for killing both their parents anytime soon.

Sarah's case went to trial in February 2005. Lead prosecutor, Jim Thomas, was confident that his team had all the forensic evidence required to convict Sarah of first-degree murder. But he was worried that they wouldn't be able to convince the jury of something so inconceivable: that someone who had all the advantages Sarah did would suddenly throw it all away and turn into a killer overnight.

Sarah's defense attorney, Robert Pangburn, still believed that Santos was somehow involved. He figured it would have been easy for Santos to recruit some of his hoodlum friends to carry out the crime, but he never questioned Santos about it. Instead, he built his whole defense on the theory that, since Sarah didn't have traces of blood on her when it had spattered on everything else, including the gun, she couldn't have possibly pulled the trigger. Then again, there was that bloody bathrobe in the garbage.

The six-week trial started in Blaine County, but it was soon moved to the Ada County Courthouse in Boise because of all the media coverage. The trial proceedings ripped apart Sarah's extended family even further and alienated her friends, since many of them were now being asked to testify against her. Eleven of her relatives took the stand, sometimes pleading and sometimes getting angry. Matt described the heated arguments that had been common between Sarah and her mother. "They didn't get along," he said. "There was constant fighting and bickering back and forth." At the end, he said, "I never want to see or hear from my sister again."

Waiting for the jury's decision was torture for Sarah's relatives. Pat Dishman, her maternal grandmother, said that it took overwhelming evidence to convince a grandmother that her daughter could have been murdered by her grand-daughter—and yet, even she had become convinced that Sarah must be guilty. The pain and sadness she felt as a result of that knowledge was indescribable to her.

"I loved my parents, and I love my family," Sarah said stoically before the sentencing, speaking in public for the first time since the start of the trial. "I am deeply grieving the loss of my parents as well as the loss of my home, my friends and my community. With the guidance of the Lord and the continued support of those that believe in me, I hope to rebuild my life and prove that I can be a productive member of society."

Thomas said that family members were disappointed in her speech. "We hoped that Sarah would truly turn to the family and talk to them," he explained, "not give this canned statement."

The jury's verdict came back guilty on both counts of first-degree murder. Judge Barry Wood wasn't any more swayed by Sarah's plea for leniency than her family was. He sentenced 18-year-old Sarah to the maximum penalty of life imprisonment for each of the crimes, to be served consecutively with no chance of parole, and an additional 15 years for using a rifle to commit the murders. Sarah listened in visible shock, holding back tears. She had spent two years in jail already…and now they were saying she'd be there for the rest of her life.

"If this case had been a death penalty one, you would have been a candidate for execution," Wood told her, but because of her age and the family involvement, prosecutors hadn't asked for it.

Pangburn had been hoping for more compassion from the judge, so he immediately said he was going to appeal Wood's decision, focusing on the long sentence and some questionable instructions Wood had given to the jury. However, Pangburn planned to ask the state public defender to help them out since Sarah had no more money. Thomas promised to send 40 boxes of documents to the Idaho attorney general lawyers, who would handle the appeal instead of him.

Right after her sentencing, Sarah was moved temporarily to another prison in Idaho, which had more suitable facilities for female prisoners. From there, she was handed over to the Pocatello Women's Correction Facility, which was run by the Idaho Department of Correction. Meanwhile, since there wasn't any further suspicion over Santos' involvement in the murders, he was deported to Mexico.

Sarah's trial had already become the costliest in Blaine County history, ringing up a price tag of over a million dollars. Pangburn had 42 days to file his appeal but ended up missing the deadline, so it was dismissed by the high court. However, by July 2006, Sarah had fired Pangburn and re-appealed her conviction to the Idaho Supreme Court, thanks to a ruling by Judge Wood that Pangburn's delay hadn't been her fault. Wood then appointed a new defense team from the State Appellate Public Defender's Office, which included attorney Sara B. Thomas instead of Blaine County public defender Stephen Thompson, as had been expected.

In her Notice of Appeal, Sarah claimed that her sentences were excessive. From an objective perspective, it might seem like getting two life sentences for taking two lives would be a pretty fair trade, but Sarah didn't see it that way.

She also said that she had been denied the right to due process of law during her trial, based on instructions that Wood had given the jury during the deliberations. He had told the jury that they could find her guilty of first-degree murder not just for pulling the trigger, but also for aiding and abetting, even though she was never charged with that. Sarah's argument was that she had a constitutional right to a unanimous decision by the jury, and that if some of the jury members thought she was only guilty of aiding and abetting the murders, while others thought she was, in fact, guilty of carrying them out, then there shouldn't have been a unanimous verdict. However, in Wood's defense, according to Idaho law, there's not a clear distinction between the two charges: murder is murder.

Of course, this little loophole meant that Pangburn's sole defense of "no blood, no guilt," which focused entirely on whether or not Sarah had pulled the trigger, had become completely moot.

On March 8, 2007, Sarah sent a handwritten memo to the Blaine County 5th District Court that said, "I am innocent of all crimes for which I was convicted. I did not kill my parents. Furthermore, I did not participate in any way in my parents' death."

Her motive this time was money. The note was written in response to her brother Matt's continued attempt to get her potential share of the $550,000 life insurance policies their parents had: $450,000 for Alan through Beneficial Life Insurance Co., and $100,000 for Diane through the Mony Life Insurance Company. Matt and Sarah were both beneficiaries in their will, and he got his half shortly after the murders. Feeling that Sarah didn't deserve any of the money, he had been trying to get her share as well.

Back in September 2005, Blaine County 5th District Judge Robert J. Elgee had ruled in Matt's favor—according to him, Sarah had no right to the money because of the Idaho Slayer's Act, which states that a murderer can't profit from the victim's estate. But two months later, he announced that the money couldn't be distributed yet, since Sarah's criminal appeal hadn't been resolved.

Then, in 2007, Matt's lawyer, Bruce Collier, filed a motion to release the funds. His argument was based on a similar case in which the Supreme Court backed an Elmore County 4th District Court ruling that a man who had been convicted of killing his wife wasn't entitled to any of her life insurance benefits. But Elgee was still hesitant to let any money be dispersed while Sarah's appeal was before the Supreme Court, and in this case, matters were more complicated because Sarah had no attorney in this civil case with her brother. In the end, Elgee released the money to Matt, contingent on the high court's approval. Because of the time and money Matt would have had to spend on lawyers to take his case to the high court, however, he opted to wait for the criminal appeal to be decided.

In June 2008, the Idaho Supreme Court rejected Sarah's appeal again, saying that Judge Wood had not mishandled the case. In fact, they said if anyone was to blame, it was Sarah's original defense attorneys, who had focused on the wrong aspect of her defense. If Pangburn's defense had revolved around proving that Sarah hadn't had any hand whatsoever in the murders instead of "no blood, no guilt," then he wouldn't have been caught off guard when Wood told the jury that Sarah could still be found guilty of first-degree murder even if she hadn't pulled the trigger. As it was, since neither the defense nor the prosecutor had brought up the possibility that someone else had been involved in the shootings, Sarah's appeal held no weight.

A few weeks later, after a three-year hiatus, the case returned to Blaine County courts, where Wood re-opened the files for a post-conviction relief petition. Sarah was asking for a new trial, and this time, her focus was on Pangburn's "ineffective legal counsel."

Coincidentally, five months earlier, Pangburn had been suspended from practicing law in Idaho for two years. It wasn't related to Sarah's case in any way, but stemmed back to when Pangburn was a lawyer in Oregon. At one point, he had been accused of "conduct involving dishonesty, fraud, deceit or misrepresentation," and he resigned from the Oregon State Bar in 2004 as a result. Resignation from a state bar, though, is just like a suspension and should have lasted longer, but Pangburn was back practicing law in Idaho in no time. The Idaho State Bar Professional Conduct Board filed a complaint against him in June 2005, shortly after Sarah's original trial ended.

Sarah's defense attorneys also tried to take the case to the U.S. Supreme Court, but the high court turned them down.

On February 19, 2009, one of Sarah's attorneys, Christopher Simms, filed a document in court revealing some new evidence—previously unidentified fingerprints found on the murder weapon that had finally been identified by the Idaho State Police Bureau of Criminal Identification. Fingerprint expert Robert J. Kerchusky, who was a consultant with the crime lab, confirmed that the prints belonged to someone who hadn't been investigated as part of the original case. Simms said that, based on this new evidence, Sarah should be allowed to have another trial.

However, investigators didn't release the identity of the person whose prints were on the gun because they said he had nothing to do with the crimes. As it turned out, he had been a former roommate of the man who had rented the guesthouse from the Johnsons. He was the tenant who had owned the murder weapon. Detectives interviewed both men and determined that the roommate had handled the rifle when they moved in and had used it at a shooting range just before the murders took place. This also corroborated what prosecutors had always argued, that Sarah had stolen the gun from the guesthouse without permission from its owner.

Jim Thomas, the prosecuting attorney, released a statement to the media immediately following this newest development. He wrote: "Investigators are confident that there is no connection between this person and Sarah Johnson. The identification of this print does nothing to lessen the guilt of Sarah Johnson, nor does it undermine the original investigation."

Nonetheless, the post-conviction process continues to go forward, and Judge Wood has agreed to allow the new evidence. Despite that gesture, Simms has asked Wood to disqualify himself from the case, saying that the judge is biased against Sarah. Wood has denied the charge and pointed out that it was the jury that had convicted Sarah, not him.

Wood was planning to retire soon anyway, and started scaling back his work, but Sarah Johnson's ongoing case is one of the few that he has kept. At the time of publication, Sarah and her attorneys were still trying to get another trial, and depending on how much longer the process stretches out, she may end up with a different judge after all.

CHAPTER THREE

Franz Edmund Creffield
The False Prophet
(1871–1906)

The worst crime is faking it.

—Kurt Cobain (1967–94), American musician and singer
of the grunge rock band Nirvana

"Anyone can experience the power of receiving messages from God," Franz Edmund Creffield preached to the small gathering that night in 1903. "Whether they doubt me or believe other teachings, it doesn't matter. And when you become worthy of this sort of personal communion with The Almighty and are receiving your own messages from God, your names will be inscribed on a Holy Roll in Heaven."

Several of the people in the audience gasped quietly and looked at one another in awe.

"But you have to hurry," Creffield went on. "There are only a limited number of spaces on the Holy Roll."

Some people watching the sermon rolled their eyes and tapped their fingers on their foreheads, indicating that they thought Creffield must be crazy. Others were falling for his tales, hook, line and sinker.

"God have mercy!" Creffield shouted.

He was met by several moments of silence as everyone took it all in. Then, finally, in a small voice, a woman whispered back, "God have mercy!"

"God will have victory tonight!" yelled Creffield.

A few people got up and walked out, but the rest knelt down in prayer.

"God will have victory tonight," they answered.

The group then embarked upon a marathon prayer session, continuing nonstop for 12 hours straight. Creffield said he could heal a woman by laying his hands on her and using his special powers, causing all the women to let loose, some shaking their heads until their hairpins fell out.

"God have mercy!" they cried, louder and louder, as they begged forgiveness for their sins.

"Any of you who believe you've sinned must seek forgiveness by lying on the floor and rolling, over and over, until your sins have been atoned for," Creffield ordered.

The people rolled and banged and stomped on the floor, clapping their hands and praying loudly, and then rolled some more, until they were completely exhausted. Most of them claimed that God had spoken to them personally, though it may have just been dizziness from all that rolling that made them delirious.

"You are now God's anointed," Creffield announced. His new followers gazed at him in amazement and admiration. After all, he had promised they could each receive messages from God, and sure enough, they had.

These people gathered around Creffield had previously been soldiers in the Salvation Army, just as he had. Since he knew what they believed in and what they had experienced, it was easy for him to offer them something completely different. Besides, convincing people who already believe in God that you have a better way to interact with Him is a lot easier than convincing people who don't believe in God that He exists. In this way, Creffield's "business" model was pretty much set.

It's hard to say whether Creffield was just faking his identity as a prophet of God—what with his magic powers and direct access to the Big Guy—or whether he truly believed it. More likely, it was a combination of both.

People who are trying to become successful in a certain area of their lives are often told by personal development teachers to "fake it 'til you make it." This credo is based on the belief that if you act like the something you want to become, then it will be that much easier to become it.

It seems like Creffield's story is one big case of faking it 'til he made it, but really, it didn't take him long to "make it," because all those Salvation Army soldiers were pretty convinced after that 12-hour super-session. Chances are Creffield convinced himself that he was really what he said he was at the same time he was convincing everyone else. Either way, his arrival in the small town of Corvallis, at the end of the Oregon Trail, launched a series of jaw-dropping capers between 1903 and 1906.

Franz Edmund Crefeld, whose name was later anglicized to Creffield, was born in 1871 in Germany and was educated in the Catholic priesthood. As a young man, he came to the United States to avoid military service and settled on the West Coast.

Creffield may have been big in charisma, but definitely not in stature—he was only five-foot-six and 135 pounds, with pale skin, light hair and blue eyes. He started preaching on street corners in 1899, while he was a soldier in the Salvation Army in Portland, Oregon.

At the time, the Salvation Army didn't have the respect it does now. People labeled its adherents as a bunch of religious crackpots, and the Army was only starting to be regarded as a reputable organization. Creffield seemed to be a good potential officer, so they sent him to Officer Training School and posted him around Oregon, in The Dalles, Oregon City, McMinnville and Heppner. But Creffield had an issue with how the Salvation Army relied on donations, and he kept arguing with other soldiers about money. As a result, he never pulled in as much cash with his big drum as his peers did.

Creffield didn't like others controlling him and wanted to do everything his own way, so what would be an admirable way out of the Salvation Army? Why, of course…receiving a message from God Himself telling him to do what he wanted to do.

In 1901, Creffield claimed he had gotten a message from God that said, "Don't solicit for money anymore and leave the Salvation Army. Its people are not entirely of God." So Creffield followed the holy instructions.

For a while he studied at the Pentecostal Mission and Training School in Salem, but then he had another revelation: he was God's Elect and was to preach a new doctrine. So off he went to Corvallis, a small farming community where everybody knew everything about everybody else.

After that first, extremely long meeting during which Creffield successfully converted several of his fellow former

Salvation Army devotees, his organization became known by a few different names. Some people called them the Come-outers, while others called them the Holy Rollers. Internally, over time, the followers would come up with an even stranger name for themselves.

But Corvallis city officials didn't like the Holy Rollers' meetings. As the number of converts grew to over a dozen women and several men, things got more and more out of hand. Creffield decided that gatherings should now be held during the day because the vibe at night wasn't right, even though that meant that most men wouldn't be able to attend. And since they had no official meeting place, they would use various members' houses, though the loud praying, rolling and strange sounds that emanated from these frequent gatherings freaked out the neighbors. Meanwhile, the Holy Rollers were making news headlines throughout the Pacific Northwest, and even in places as far away as Scotland.

By the summer of 1903, Creffield had been barred from holding meetings within city limits. No problem, though, because he was very resourceful…he simply relocated the whole shebang to the nearby uninhabited Smith Island for a months-long campout that was truly wild.

While most men continued to work, many of their wives and daughters went to live with Creffield on the island. They included 23-year-old Donna Mitchell Starr and her 15-year-old sister, Esther Mitchell, as well as Donna's sister-in-law, Hattie Baldwin Starr, and Hattie's niece, Una Baldwin. There was also 22-year-old Attie Bray—niece of Donna's and Hattie's husbands, Burgess and Clarence Starr—and Attie's friend, 27-year-old Rose Seeley, as well as Rose's siblings, 28-year-old Edna, 19-year-old Wesley and

16-year-old Florence. Then there was 23-year-old Maud
Hurt, a long-time religious fanatic who had been trying to
convert people to Christianity since the age of eight, as well
as her mother, Sarah Starr Hurt, sister of Burgess and
Clarence, and Maud's 16-year-old sister, Mae. Other
followers included 35-year-old logger Sampson Levins,
a former Methodist who had become disenchanted; Sophie
Hartley and her fiancé, Lee Campbell, who were previously
not that interested in religion; Sophie's mother, 44-year-old
Cora Hartley, wife of one of the richest men in Corvallis,
Lewis Hartley; 22-year-old Mollie Sandell and her 26-year-old
sister, Olive, two former Methodists from a wealthy family
who had recently joined the Salvation Army; and Mollie's
fiancé, 21-year-old Frank Hurt, brother of Maud and Mae.
Frank actually left his job as a shipping clerk at Portland's
Ainsworth Dock to go to Smith Island for the summer.

Burgess and Clarence Starr didn't camp out with the Holy
Rollers, but they did hang around them a fair deal because the
couple was on the island fulfilling a wood-cutting contract.
Maud Hurt's fiancé, James Berry, a successful 24-year-old businessman who owned a bicycle shop, also visited a few times.

"Our religion means the restoration of all things," Creffield
preached to his flock when they arrived on the island. "The
world will be destroyed by fire, and a new world will be
born, where only peace will reign. It will be like the Garden
of Eden, where everything's the same as the beginning of the
world, and there will be no sin." But wasn't the Garden of Eden
supposed to be the place where the original sin took place?

"I am now Joshua, the Holy Prophet," Creffield continued.
"In the future, I will become Elijah, the Restorer. I am to lead

the 12 tribes of Israel back to Jerusalem for the restoration of all things, and the millennium will dawn on earth."

Frank Hurt's jaw dropped. "Our leader is an apostle," he exclaimed. "Just like those mentioned in the Bible!"

Prayer services on the island were so long that a 12-hour session was now considered relatively short; the average length was 24 hours. It might seem inconceivable that a religious service could go that long, but it bears remembering that these weren't typical services. They consisted of a lot of frenzied wailing, groaning, singing, stomping, clapping and, of course, rolling around on the ground.

When James Berry came to visit the group on the island, he was astounded to see that they had become more frantic than ever. They explained to him that they were excited because God had told them their prayers for a new tabernacle were about to be answered, and that it was going to be built right away.

"How are you going to pay for it?" Berry asked.

"We're not—you are," they answered. "God told us so."

Admittedly, Berry had liked Creffield's ideas when he had first heard them, but he had already lent him some money to get his church going. That loan was now long past due, and Berry hadn't been paid back even a penny of it.

"Well, when might I expect payment for the loan I already made to you?" Berry asked.

"I talked with God about that," Creffield told him. "That loan's been canceled, so you should write me a receipt saying it's been paid in full."

Berry was incredulous.

"You're also supposed to shut down your business, sell everything of value—including that new automobile you purchased, which is from carnal hands—give the money to me and devote yourself to the church," Creffield informed a dumbfounded Berry.

"Either you or God made a mistake," Berry answered, "because you're not getting another cent from me."

"God will smite you for this!" Creffield roared. "How dare you anger God!"

Before long, Creffield ordered Maud to call off her engagement to Berry. She did, telling Berry that it was a command from God.

Interestingly—and hypocritically, as it turned out—Creffield now started preaching about personal purity and the evils of fornication.

"Are you still in bondage to your carnal nature?" he asked them. "Do not be discouraged. God wants to cleanse you, to purge you from your inbred sin and baptize you with fire!"

And it wasn't just fornication that was bad, according to Creffield. He told Lee Campbell and Sophie Hartley that they needed to call off their engagement, too, because the relationship between a man and his wife was "unholy." But before he got a chance to tell Frank Hurt and Mollie Sandell the same thing, they eloped and were married in a private ceremony.

Even though she was newly married, Mollie, like all the other women in the flock, soon discovered that she was still eligible to be "endowed with the grace of love" by Creffield. Apparently God told him he should perform this ceremony with each of his female followers, whereby a long prayer service took place in the privacy of his tent, followed by a kissing session. "You're carnal and of the devil!" he would yell at any woman who refused. The jury is still out on whether or not fornication actually took place.

By this time, some of the men who had previously been okay with their wives and sisters hanging around Creffield began to have their doubts about this whole Holy Roller thing. Burgess Starr told his brother, Clarence, that he thought some of Creffield's actions were bordering on criminal, and he wasn't sure anymore if he really was an apostle. When Creffield found out, he fought back in the best way he knew how.

"God has revealed to me that Burgess Starr is insincere in his faith and must be shunned!" Creffield announced. But his accusations didn't stop there—all the men except Frank Hurt, Lee Campbell and Sampson Levins were labeled insincere nonbelievers and shunned. These "shunned" men quickly found out that being shunned also meant that their Holy Roller wives wanted nothing to do with them.

It was unbelievable how these people mindlessly followed Creffield around like lemmings. He abused them and called them names, but they didn't care. Part of it might have been that they were exhausted from the day-long prayer sessions and half-starved from barely eating anything besides some stolen peaches—a combination that can affect anyone's ability to think rationally.

Now, despite Creffield's intended persona as a revered holy man, his non-followers started calling him a "Satanic influence."

The Salvation Army wanted to do their part to rescue the misguided Holy Rollers from Creffield since many of them used to be Salvation Army soldiers, so they sent 11-year veteran Captain Charles Brooks to save them. Unfortunately, their plan backfired despite Brooks' briefings and his motivational talks with Salvation Army founder General William Booth beforehand. Instead of rescuing the congregation, Brooks decided to join Creffield's church, throwing his uniform into the campfire and announcing that he was also a prophet. He soon became Creffield's right-hand man and his most trusted disciple.

When the summer came to an end and the chilly, rainy weather arrived, the Holy Rollers knew they couldn't stay camped out on the island any longer. But they couldn't return to Corvallis, since they were still banned from holding their meetings within the city. Their prayers were finally answered, but not by God. Maud and Sarah Hurt invited 20 Holy Rollers, including Creffield and Brooks, to move into their house, which was just outside the city limits. Sarah's husband and Maud's father, Victor Hurt, let it happen, mainly because he had no idea what he was in for.

Creffield, as any good prophet would, made sure that his followers did exactly what he said, or they couldn't be his followers anymore. He ran a tight, somewhat illogical ship. Besides making them roll and groan for hours on end, he insisted that they stop using lights, candles or anything other than daylight to see by. He also told them they weren't allowed to eat anything he hadn't sanctified by touching it with his hands, and then he refused to sanctify anything but bread and water for a week so they could experience hunger. Sometimes he made them all sleep together on the floor with hardly any clothes on so they could experience the cold. And he told them they weren't allowed to associate with infidels, even if they were family members or spouses.

The problem with living in the Hurts' home was that Victor, at first, refused to join the church. Since that made him an infidel, they started calling him the Black Devil and told him over and over again that God would smite him.

Sarah Hurt's brother, Burgess Starr, came to the house to visit his wife, Donna, but Creffield ordered her not to touch him. Then Warren Hartley tried to convince his sister and mother, Sophie and Cora, to come home, but they seemed spaced out in a trance and said they weren't allowed to leave unless Creffield said it was okay. Warren sent a message to his father, Lewis, who was off mining, and Lewis was livid. He had attended Creffield's early gatherings but always thought the preacher was harmless, if not a little nuts.

When Lewis came to get his wife and daughter, Cora told him to go away because Creffield had taught them that marriage was unholy. This didn't seem like Cora. Lewis had heard the ghastly rumors and had to find out the truth.

"Are there orgies taking place here?" he asked his wife.

"No," Cora said. She had never lied to her husband before, and she may have been telling the truth then, but it would only be a matter of time.

Victor kept coming and going between work and home, trying to keep up a normal life while ignoring the loud and rambunctious prayer sessions taking place daily in his living room. Finally, on October 28, he gave in and joined the Holy Rollers. He sent a letter of resignation to the mercantile shop where he worked, along with his keys, stating that he had been living in sin but was now going to devote himself to the work of God. Then he posted signs all along the front of the house that read: "Positively no admittance except on God's business."

The next day, a thorough housecleaning took place at the Hurt residence. While it might be normal to do a complete

cleaning at least twice a year, this time was anything but normal. Creffield instructed his followers to take all of the Hurts'
furniture outside and set it on fire. Then he made them burn
all their belongings—heirlooms, photos, knick-knacks,
kitchen utensils, dishes, guns, appliances—"because they were
received from carnal hands." Next, the Holy Rollers ripped
out the wooden walks, flowers, shrubs and trees outside, and
threw those in the fire. Finally, as a warped sacrificial gesture,
they burned some small animals alive—an entire flock of
chickens and the pet dog and cat.

Cora and Sophie Hartley went to their house, smashed all
their china and hauled everything they had left—everything
that hadn't already been sold to raise money for Creffield—
back to the fire to be burned, too. Then a second fire was
started at the Starr's house.

These events had Victor Hurt's friends knocking on his
door to talk some sense into him, especially when they heard
that the Hurt's recently adopted baby, Martha, may have
been sacrificed in the fire as well. But Creffield and Brooks
wouldn't let anyone in the house, so Sheriff M.P. Burnett,
along with Deputy Henderson and Deputy Attorney E.R.
Bryson, tried their luck and managed to slip by Creffield
while he was consulting God over whether or not they were
welcome.

They found the Holy Rollers on the floor, praying, laughing
and crying, and looking gaunt and pale. Happily, baby
Martha was there, too, alive and unharmed.

Frank Hurt tried to explain to the lawmen, "We burned
the furniture to make more room for meetings…and we
burned some trinkets, because we don't believe people who
have been saved should have luxuries." When asked about

burning the pets, Frank admitted, "Yes, we killed them…but only because we had tried to get rid of them, and they came back. You don't find anything like pets in the Bible, and the Bible is our law."

Victor wouldn't admit it then, but in truth, Sarah had already abandoned baby Martha, leaving Victor to care for her, and the sacrifice had almost happened. It all stemmed from Creffield's skewed teachings.

We already know that Creffield's followers had to be devout and do whatever he said, or he'd have them "shunned." But seriously, why did they care? What was it that made them follow such crazy orders without seeing that the whole thing was absolutely insane and that Creffield was likely insane too? What's even more mind-blowing is that these people were previously very normal and respected members of Corvallis.

All cults follow a few principles of mind control in various combinations, and in hindsight, Creffield's "church" was most certainly a cult. Whether he studied it beforehand or not, Creffield employed a lot of these principles. First, members are prepared for thought control through subliminal suggestions, which usually take the form of excessive repetition and extended verbal, visual, audio or tactile drills—the long rolling and groaning sessions covered all that. Thought control can also be facilitated through decreased sleep and nutrition, which Creffield accomplished by making his followers sleep half-naked on the floor and only letting them eat what he had sanctified.

Next, the cult's environment is strictly controlled in order to keep its followers isolated; Creffield did this by holing his flock up, first on the island, and then in the Hurts' house.

Then, it's made clear that God is not only present in the organization, but punishment will come to anyone who dares to leave. Creffield accomplished this with all his talk of receiving messages from God and "shunning" and "smiting" all the infidels. Finally, the followers' freedom of choice is removed by making the world seem black and white or divided into good and evil. Creffield did this by saying that only the Holy Rollers would appear on Heaven's Holy Roll and that followers couldn't associate with non-believers, who were aligned with the devil.

Typically, cult members are also encouraged to confess their sins, and Holy Rollers did so during their marathon prayer sessions. In all cases, the cult leader is to be held in reverence and is depicted as knowing the absolute truth, and Creffield definitely accomplished that. Add in that Creffield's followers had been actively searching for religious salvation prior to Creffield's ministry, and that they were also seeing immediate social proof—with their friends and family taking part—and you've got a dangerous mixture.

Unfortunately, as there was no specific law in Corvallis against burning cats and dogs, the police couldn't legally do anything with the pyromaniacs at the Hurts' house. However, they did take Creffield and Brooks in to test their sanity.

By no means were they found to be completely sound, but they were diagnosed as too sane to be committed to an asylum against their will. And although they admitted that they'd probably kill someone if God ordered it—He had never done so yet, and they didn't foresee it happening any time soon—Henderson still had to let them go. He advised the men to leave town, since there had been talk of tarring and feathering going around.

That night, the Hurts' house was stoned by the citizens of Corvallis, and the next day, Creffield and Brooks took off, as Henderson had suggested. But Frank Hurt couldn't leave well enough alone, and he insisted they both come back to his father's house.

In mid-November, work began on enlarging the house into a tabernacle, and Victor was taken on a trip to Portland by James Berry, his daughter's "shunned" fiancé. Once he was away from the insane goings-on, Victor's own sanity started to return. For a week, he examined Creffield's agenda from all angles and decided that he wanted nothing more to do with it. On his return, he kicked Creffield and Brooks out of his house.

But the rest of the Hurts were still enamored with Creffield, so Frank rented a house with his wife, Mollie, just outside the Corvallis city limits and invited the Holy Rollers to shack up there.

During this time, Creffield announced that he was going to marry 16-year-old Esther Mitchell, which prompted her older sister, Phoebe, to ship her off to the Boys and Girls Aid Society in Portland to get her away from Creffield. There, they labeled Esther as deranged, since she kept shouting, "Hallelujah! Glory to God!" over and over, as well as rolling on the floor and praying for hours on end. When her brothers, Perry and George, came to visit her, she didn't even recognize them. George was so worried about her that he stopped eating and sleeping.

"If you don't watch it, you'll become as nutty as the Holy Rollers," Perry told his brother.

By December, Creffield claimed to be receiving new messages from God. He told them, "Holy people need not wear clothing," as he stripped down to the buff. "Clothing was intended to cover up sin and shame," he went on. So what did his loyal followers do? They took off all their clothes, too, and joined Creffield in chanting and rolling on the floor buck-naked…all except for Wesley Seeley, who had finally had enough and left.

The rest of the Holy Rollers kept on rolling for hours, and then Creffield said he could at last reveal his true mission to them: to find the woman who would be the mother of the second Christ. The Holy Rollers, he said, would now be known as the Brides of Christ, and one of the women would be chosen. But first, they all had to be sanctified so they could be virgins again in God's eyes.

Creffield assured them that their compliance couldn't be considered an act of lust, because as Brides of Christ, they were all incapable of sinning. Instead, this was all about free love. And just like that, Christmas season became orgy season at Frank's house. Every single one of the women made love to Creffield, even in front of their daughters, sisters and mothers. Sarah Hurt held out the longest, but on threat of eternal damnation, finally submitted.

After making love to all the women—some of whom had been real virgins beforehand—Creffield announced that the chosen mother of the second Christ was Esther Mitchell, who was still locked up in Portland. She was also the only true virgin left.

Esther's other sister, Donna Starr, visited her and excitedly told her the news; shortly thereafter, she and Frank tried to abduct Esther from the institution. When they failed, Esther was put on a train to Illinois to live with her biological father, who had deserted the family when Esther was six.

Could sex have been Creffield's main motivation all along? Or was it about money? It's hard to imagine he made very much from Berry's loan or from the belongings his followers sold off for him; but then again, they were completely dedicated to giving him anything he wanted, so why would Creffield need money? And that brings us to a third possible motivation: power. Creffield was certainly experiencing plenty of that. But the one sure thing that comes with power is someone who wants to take it away.

On January 4, 1904, 20 men gathered together and dubbed themselves the White Caps. They stormed over to Frank's house, broke down the door, and as the women sat and sang blithely, they kidnapped the men that were there—Creffield, Brooks, Levins and Campbell. The White Caps bound them with rope and marched them all to a bridge on Main Street, where they told Creffield and Brooks to take off their clothes.

"Let us pray," Creffield said. "Forgive them, for they know not what they do." Then he stood there, naked and trembling, as he and Brooks were completely coated with a layer of pine tar and covered with feathers. The other two men had only the tops of their heads tarred and feathered.

Frank wasn't home when the White Caps broke in, but he watched the action from a distance and caught up with Creffield afterwards to take him home. He spent the rest of the evening removing the tar from Creffield's body.

The next day, Creffield married his second choice for a bride: Maud Hurt. The couple laid low for a while, and by March, Creffield seemed to have vanished. Maud was back living in her parents' house again, claiming she wanted nothing more to do with him.

Meanwhile, Creffield was in Portland, carrying out purification rituals with Donna Starr, his new wife's aunt by marriage, who had been moved there for safekeeping by her husband, Burgess. As Burgess had hoped, Donna had initially reverted to being the "good" wife and mother she had once been as soon as she was away from the Brides of Christ, but she soon went back to her old Holy Roller ways.

Burgess, thinking the worse, charged Creffield with adultery, a criminal offense that could land him in prison for up to two years. Twelve other men whose wives had been associated with Creffield followed suit, but District Attorney John Manning said he needed some tangible proof, or at least a written claim from any one of the husbands, that he had caught Creffield and his wife in the act. None of them admitted that they had, or else Creffield would have already been beaten to a bloody pulp. So, instead, they had Donna sign an affidavit stating that she had had improper relations with him—something she only did because they told her to, not because she actually read the piece of paper. However, before Creffield could be arrested, he vanished again.

With Creffield gone, the 17 Holy Rollers still living in Frank's house didn't come to their senses right away as everyone expected. Instead, they carried on, placing even more rigorous restrictions on themselves, based on their literal interpretations of Bible verses. Eventually, with everyone around them thinking they were going crazy because of their strange behavior—like only eating one type of food per meal or walking around barefoot with wild, tangled hair, praying in dark closets and flipping pictures to the wall—it was decided that since Creffield couldn't be found to break his spell, the Holy Rollers had to be committed, one by one, to the Oregon State Insane Asylum in Salem. So that was what they did, with Sarah Hurt being the last to go, kicking and screaming.

It turns out the reason Sarah put up such a fuss was because Creffield had been hiding under their porch the whole time, and she and Maud had secretly been feeding him. After they were committed to the asylum, he stayed there alone, naked and without food, for over a month. Then, on July 29, he was found by Roy, the Hurts' 14-year-old adopted son, who was looking for worms.

Even though he was still in his early 30s, the man who crawled out from the hole looked about 60; he was pale, emaciated and barely able to stand, with gray hair and a beard.

"I am Elijah!" he announced, causing those watching to snicker.

When asked why he risked starvation to stay hidden for so long, Creffield replied, "The Lord told me to hide away, and I was crucified while I was there. God told me to suffer for my people and to die from hunger and cold."

But before suffering, he continued to have sex with the women, coming out from under the porch while Victor was working to conduct prayer sessions and purification rituals—or, rather, orgies—in the Hurts' house. Some of the participants, like Mae Hurt and Florence Seeley, were only 16 years old, and if he had been charged for having sex with them, he would have gone to prison for a very long time, or been killed by other inmates. But Victor, who was afraid of bad publicity and public humiliation—as if he hadn't had enough already—didn't prosecute Creffield after he found out.

Still wanted for Burgess' original charge of adultery, however, Creffield was taken to the Benton County Jail, where he spent the day sleeping and muttering about Jesus. Dr. Pernot, who had been part of the team that evaluated his sanity in November, examined him again and this time diagnosed him as demented.

Since Detective Hartman, from Portland, had been searching for Creffield for four months with no luck, he wanted to be the one to get some press for bringing him back alive. So he concocted a story about angry mobs trying to snatch Creffield from under his nose to make the arrest sound more incredible than it actually was. In reality, the Starr brothers had thought about stirring something up but were talked out of it by Victor, who wanted the law to take its proper course. And despite reports to the contrary, the crowds that gathered at every train station along the line were just trying to get a peek at Creffield, the head Holy Roller, and weren't there to lynch him.

"I expect to be killed," Creffield told Hartman upon being warned that a violent crowd would probably greet them in Portland. "Men who are not understood are always killed, and if the Lord commands it, it shall be so."

As promised, there was a crowd of a thousand or so waiting for them, but the weakened Creffield was escorted through without incident. Then he was taken to his own cell in the Multnomah County Jail, where he promptly fell asleep.

When taken to court for his arraignment, Creffield pleaded "not guilty" to the charge of adultery. Then he declined an attorney, saying, "I don't need a lawyer. God will plead my case."

He could have been bailed out for $2000, but since Creffield apparently had no money, he stayed in jail for six weeks awaiting his trial. During that time, he charmed his fellow inmates and the guards with his famous charisma. Soon, he was being called a model prisoner and was being treated with respect, which was a 180-degree turn from their attitude a few days prior.

Meanwhile, the Holy Rollers who were in the asylum heard the gossip about Creffield's arrest from the other patients—the authorities hadn't told them directly, since they figured the patients would think it was a trick. Now, instead of taking the news as proof that Creffield was just a plain old mortal as the doctors had hoped, Creffield's flock saw it as a sign that God was rescuing him from starvation and became even more devoted to their faith.

On September 16, 1904, Creffield's trial began. Donna Starr testified that she had indeed committed adultery, based on God's instructions.

"It was to purge my soul of devils," she matter-of-factly told the court. Several other former Holy Rollers took the stand and told of seeing kissing and sex taking place before their eyes, and the tales of the wild orgies were finally made public.

When it was Creffield's turn on the stand, he didn't call any witnesses and said the Bible would be his defense. He read various passages from the book, asking the judge and jury to follow along. Then, despite his original plea of "not guilty," he admitted that, "In the eyes of this world, I am guilty, but God is on my side."

Judge Alfred F. Sears figured the jury might just find Creffield to be insane, but after only 20 minutes of deliberation, jury foreman Jacob Spiegl gave the verdict:

"Guilty." While most convicted criminals would show anger, sadness or disbelief, Creffield just smiled. Judge Sears gave him the longest allowable sentence: two years in the Oregon State Penitentiary.

Now that he was behind bars, the rest of the Holy Rollers were released from their institutions; Esther Mitchell returned to Oregon, and Maud's parents forced her to legally divorce Creffield.

On December 13, 1905, after serving 17 months of his sentence, working on the road gang and chalking up points for good behavior, Creffield was released from prison. Now he had a third religious identity: he was the new Christ. He said that God had told him that Christ wouldn't be reborn from a new mother after all; instead, his prison time had represented the crucifixion (a second one, since he had also claimed to be crucified under the porch), and he was now arisen.

Frank and Mollie Hurt, coerced by Mollie's parents, had since moved to Seattle with their new baby daughter, Ruth. Creffield went there to stay with them and sent for Maud, who revealed that they were no longer married. But it wasn't a problem; they just got married again, on April 3, 1906.

Creffield then determined that the Holy Rollers should create a new Eden on the Yachats River, a wild area near where the Hurt kids had been born, and announced that all the Brides of Christ had to go there immediately. "I have called the wrath of God upon the modern Sodoms of Corvallis, Portland, Seattle…and San Francisco," he said. "Anyone who doesn't come to the new Eden is in danger." Why he included San Francisco in his list of condemned cities is anyone's guess, but there it was.

On April 18, San Francisco was almost completely leveled by an earthquake. Creffield took credit for it, and his followers became more dedicated to him than ever. As the Holy Rollers got ready to head for the Yachats River on the Oregon coast, Frank quit his new job as an engineer on a steamship, took $300 from his savings and started packing up his family: Mollie, Ruth, Maud and Mollie's sister, Olive.

Just before sneaking off to join the others, Donna Starr had been very affectionate with Burgess. He was convinced that she was finally done with the Holy Rollers, since she had told him that she was sorry for everything and didn't know why she had done what Creffield told her to. But then he woke up one night and discovered that Donna had left, abandoning him and their three children: five-year-old Gertrude, three-year-old Rachel and seven-month-old Clifford. She ended up walking the last 80 miles to the coast, since she didn't have enough money to pay for the whole journey.

Meanwhile, George Mitchell was sick in the hospital with the measles and a high fever, and during that time, he claimed to be getting messages from God himself—but His messages were telling him to kill Creffield. At the same time, when Lewis Hartley discovered that his wife and daughter Cora and Sophie were heading to the coast to reunite with Creffield, he also tried to kill the cult leader. While Creffield and some of his followers were boarding a ferry, Hartley shot at him from the dock, but his gun misfired because he had loaded it with the wrong cartridges.

"See, no man can kill me," Creffield shouted as Hartley stood agape. "I am indestructible!" And the flock believed him.

They camped on the Yachats River but were told to move on by neighbors who didn't appreciate the Holy Rollers stripping down and burning their clothes in an effort to live more like Adam and Eve. So the group moved to Ten Mile Creek, where Creffield announced that he was going to look for a better spot to establish the new Eden, and that Maud should meet him in Seattle after he did so. The rest of the Holy Rollers tried staying with Attie Bray's parents, who lived nearby, but they were all turned away—even Attie herself. So they set up camp at the remote Cummins Creek to wait for Creffield.

When George discovered that Creffield and Maud were going to be in Seattle, he went there, too. He walked around for five days looking for them, until finally, on May 7, 1906, he spotted Maud and Creffield walking arm in arm down the street. They had stopped in front of a drugstore so Maud could weigh herself, and George walked right up behind them and shot Creffield point blank in the back of his head.

Creffield fell to the ground at Maud's feet, not crucified, but most definitely dead.

Most stories might end here. This one doesn't.

Maud started freaking out after her husband was shot, trying to hit George and yelling, "He didn't harm you!"

Normally Maud carried a pistol—luckily this was the one time she'd left it at home—and if she had had it, George would have surely been shot, too. George grabbed her wrists to stop her flailing and then let her go as she dropped to the ground.

She cradled Creffield's head, muttering, "They can't kill Joshua!" But shortly afterwards, Maud calmed down and began telling people that Creffield would rise from the dead in three days, just as Christ had. Apparently this was to be his third resurrection, but it never happened.

George stayed calmly at the scene, smoking a cigar and waiting to be arrested. Then, on June 25, the most sensational and expensive trial in Washington history began. The proceedings attracted so many people that spectators overflowed from the courtroom into the hallway. It took four days to choose a group of jurors that was acceptable to both sides, because so many people were biased against Creffield and what he had stood for.

Many of the members of the flock who had been camping in the woods and waiting for Creffield's return came to Seattle for the trial. George Hodges, a timber cruiser, had happened upon the half-starving bunch on the beach. When he found out they were the Holy Rollers, he informed them Creffield was dead, but they didn't believe it was possible. Nobody who lived nearby would take them in, not even temporarily, but eventually Hodges contacted Victor, who enlisted a couple of men to pick them all up and take them back to his house.

During George's six-hour prosecution, it was well established that he had calmly and deliberately carried out Creffield's assassination. But the defense argued, somewhat predictably, that he had been insane at the time because of what Creffield had done to his sisters, Esther Mitchell and Donna Starr. Both of them were present at the trial, but they were there to support Creffield, not George.

The jury deliberated for just under 90 minutes and came back with their verdict: "Not guilty." Much of the audience went against courtroom protocol, applauding and cheering the verdict. George, who had become something of a local hero, shook hands with all the jurors, as well as with the adoring female fans who rushed after him as he left the courthouse. Then he politely said, "Goodbye, boys!" to the sheriff and deputies who had watched over him in jail for the past two months.

Two days later, on July 12, 1906, George and his brothers, Perry and Fred, were at the train station, about to head back to Oregon. Fred had asked Esther to make up with George, so the brothers were happy to see her come by and shake George's hand. As the four walked together, though, Esther pulled out a revolver and shot her brother George in the back of the head—in exactly the same place he had shot Creffield. Also like George, she calmly awaited her arrest. So did Maud, who had purchased the gun for Esther after George's acquittal, and they called the police from a grocery store to confess. Neither of them showed any remorse at George's death, and Maud later testified that her husband's spirit had told her to do it, and God had given the same message to Esther.

Police Chief Charles Wappenstein said, "I wish these Oregon people would kill each other on their own side of the Columbia River." Judge Archibald Frater, who had presided over George's trial, wanted to ship the two women back to the insane asylum in Salem, but the State Supreme Court wouldn't allow it. On November 17, while they were being held at the county jail awaiting trial, Maud killed herself with some strychnine she had smuggled in, and she died in Esther's arms. Esther said Maud would only do such a thing if the order had come directly from God. Two months later, Esther was sent to the Washington State Insane Asylum in Steilacoom, where she stayed for two years.

After her release, she moved to Waldport, Oregon, along with many of the other former Holy Rollers, and stayed with Maud's parents. Her new home was near where Creffield had wanted to build his new Eden. In April 1914, Esther married

James Berry, Maud's former fiancé. Then finally, four months later, on August 2, at the age of 26, she followed in Maud's footsteps again and killed herself with strychnine.

CHAPTER FOUR

Keith Hunter Jesperson
The Happy Face Killer
(1955–)

Where crime is taught from early years, it becomes a part of nature.

—Publius Ovidius Naso, a.k.a. Ovid (43 BC–18 AD),
Roman poet

The pretty 23-year-old girl introduced herself by giving him a big bear hug. "Hi, I'm Taunja!" she chirped. The hug wasn't an act of affection so much as just the way Taunja Bennett always behaved—totally trusting and unaware that everybody in the world wasn't as innocent as she was—and the regulars at the B & I Tavern in Portland, Oregon, thought nothing of it.

Keith Hunter Jesperson had been watching her all evening from the bar, and now they were standing together at the pool tables where Taunja had been checking out a game.

"Can I buy you a drink?" Jesperson asked.

"Sure!" Bennett answered enthusiastically. She had been alternating between beer and coolers all night, unable to decide between one or the other. What was one more drink? Her judgment was certainly off by now, though her friends and family later said that she was slightly mentally challenged, which made her pretty agreeable at the best of times. Either way, this hulk-like, six-foot-six, 240-pound, 35-year-old stranger towering over her didn't seem to worry her in the slightest.

Jesperson himself had been called mentally slow more than once in his life. When he graduated from high school, his IQ had been measured at 102—ranked 161 in a class of 174—and his grades had always averaged C or below. But, whether because of a mental kinship or not, he later said that Bennett's slowness excited him.

It was January 23, 1990, a typical cold, damp Tuesday in Portland. Bennett had been bored and was looking for some friends to hang out with, so she had been at the tavern all afternoon. Meeting someone new hadn't been in the plan, but why not?

Soon, however, Jesperson disappeared for a while, not telling anyone where he went. When he came back, Bennett was standing outside. "Hey, you wanna get some dinner with me?" Jesperson asked.

"Okay," she replied, as Jesperson looked through his wallet.

"Oh…I don't have enough money on me," he said. "But I've got more at home. It's not very far, will you come with me?"

But as you might've guessed, getting more money wasn't Jesperson's goal; getting Bennett alone, and away from people who knew her, was. Once they got to his place, he persuaded her to have sex instead. How much force it took him to convince her is unclear, but with Bennett's easygoing nature, it probably wasn't too difficult. It was only later that things got ugly.

Jesperson had been carrying around pent-up anger his whole life. He was born on April 6, 1955, in Chilliwack, BC, to Les and Gladys Jesperson. Despite his protests, they moved to a trailer park in Selah, Washington, when he was 12. Keith was the middle of five children—the odd man out—with an older brother and sister, and a younger brother and sister. He had an ongoing love-hate relationship with his father, a dominating man with little respect for women or kids, and who had always ridiculed Keith and his siblings, though Keith later claimed that he had been a target more than the others. The ridicule continued with Keith's schoolmates, who mocked him for his large size, withdrawn demeanor and poor grades.

Whatever the cause, Jesperson's anger was always simmering just below the surface, and it didn't just boil up—it exploded violently. But instead of confronting the people who provoked it, Jesperson usually lashed out at the defenseless, like small animals, and now Bennett.

Before he had even pulled up his pants, Jesperson was taunting Bennett with cruel remarks, and she retaliated with insults of her own. Their argument got physical when Jesperson started hitting Bennett. She tried to defend herself, but he was much bigger and stronger and hit her over 20 times in the head and face before letting up. Then, without even thinking, Jesperson grabbed her throat with one hand, a rope with the other and wrapped the latter around the former, strangling her to death.

It was Jesperson's first murder, but it wasn't the first time he had thought about it—not in the least. The first time had been when he was about 10 years old and was caught fighting with his playmate, Martin, who had a habit of getting into trouble and blaming it on Jesperson. Jesperson had beat Martin unconscious and probably would have killed him if his father hadn't intervened.

A couple of years later, a school bully had held his head under the water while they were swimming in the lake, causing him to pass out. Later, when Jesperson saw the same boy at the swimming pool, he enacted his revenge…and would have drowned him for real if a lifeguard hadn't pulled him off.

And then there were all the times as a boy that he had cruelly tortured and killed small animals. It seemed to win his father's approval—after all, the first time that Jesperson had killed a cat with his bare hands, at about six years of age, his dad had bragged about it to all his friends.

Jesperson later said that his father's reaction had prompted him to want to kill again. Sometimes it was gophers, sometimes it was crows, but often it was cats and small dogs. He moved onto bigger dogs only after his father shot Duke, his Labrador retriever. Because Jesperson was a lonely teenager, Duke had been his only friend, and the dog's death devastated him. His dad defended the action by saying that Duke looked sick, like he had gotten into some poison. Jesperson took the anger over that incident and redirected it onto other animals.

Later, when 20-year-old Jesperson—newly married to 18-year-old waitress Rose Pernick—was helping his father run the Silver Spur Mobile Park in Yakima, Washington, it was his job to kill all the stray dogs and cats that wandered onto the property. And the more his father encouraged and applauded it, the more Jesperson enjoyed it. He kept up his morbid habit well into his late 20s and early 30s, even when he and Rose were parents to three kids. He would torture his children's pets and even kill cats right in front of them. Eventually, Jesperson started to wonder what it would be like to kill a human, displaying that same twisted curiosity that prompted other people who started off maiming or killing animals to become murderers.

Now that he had killed his first person, however, Jesperson said he didn't look for animals to mistreat anymore—he looked for more people to kill.

By this time, he had split up with his wife and was working as a long-haul trucker for a company based in Cheney, Washington. His dream had always been to become an officer for the Royal Canadian Mounted Police, but he was forced to give that up after an accident in high school. Jesperson had been on the wrestling team, and his teammates always teased him about not being able to climb the rope that hung from the ceiling. One day, he decided to prove to them that he could make it to the top, but just as he made it halfway up, the rope pulled out of the bracket, dropping him 25 feet to the floor. He fell hard, hitting the side of his head and spraining his ankle—an injury that didn't heal for years.

For some reason, it's not uncommon among criminals to have wanted to be a cop at some point in their lives. Maybe it's for the danger, the thrills and the license to kill. Or perhaps they start out with good intentions, and then when they don't succeed, it becomes a case of "If you can't beat the criminals, you might as well join them."

Jesperson's marriage had always been shaky, since he didn't really like the idea of monogamy, and when he started working as a trucker, the relationship only went further downhill. He was rarely at home, and there were plenty of women hanging around truck stops looking for casual sex. Jesperson liked to call them "lot lizards."

In 1988, he found a new girlfriend named Peggy and told Rose he wanted a divorce. As Rose and the kids moved out, Jesperson and Peggy started driving together, but it quickly turned into another rocky relationship, filled with arguments over Peggy's driving skills and repeated breakups. In January 1990, Peggy decided that it was over for good this time and took off to Knoxville to see an old boyfriend. When Jesperson headed to the B & I Tavern on January 23, a couple of weeks later, he was not only bored but still angry about the breakup.

After Jesperson killed Bennett, he went back to the tavern to create an alibi, sitting calmly while he drank a few beers and chatting amiably with the other patrons. Then he returned to his rental house, put Bennett's half-dressed body in the front seat of his orange '74 Chevy Nova and drove east out of Portland towards the Columbia River Gorge. He found a dark, secluded place near Crown Point and dumped her body over an embankment, but not before cutting the button fly off her jeans in case he had left his fingerprints on it. Driving away, he tossed her Walkman out the window and then headed to a truck stop near Troutdale to drink coffee all night, establishing another alibi. At daybreak, he drove up the Sandy River Highway and threw Bennett's purse into the brush.

Later that day, a cyclist came across Taunja's body, which had tumbled down into a ditch, and called the police. They had problems identifying the body, so they listed her as a Jane Doe, but they could tell that she had been strangled to death. The story didn't make front-page news, but ended up buried in the back of papers and at the end of TV newscasts, so it took over a week for Bennett's sobbing mother to positively identify her. She confirmed that her daughter had left home just after lunch on January 23 to head to the B & I Tavern, and she hadn't seen her since.

Since bar staff and patrons vaguely remembered that Bennett had played pool that day with a couple of blonde guys, police focused their investigation on them. But soon, out of the blue, a woman came forward and confessed to the crime. Laverne Pavlinac, a 57-year-old grandmother, didn't look like a stereotypical murderer, but she was a true crime and mystery junkie and knew how a police investigation operated. After taking in as much about the story as she could from the media, Pavlinac figured this would be as good a way as any to end an abusive 10-year relationship with her live-in boyfriend, 43-year-old John Sosnovske. She figured it was okay to go to jail for a while in order to earn complete freedom from him later.

So she concocted a tale about how Sosnovske had killed Bennett and had made Pavlinac help him dispose of the body. Then she added that she had been forced to hold Bennett down, with a rope tied around her neck, while Sosnovske raped her. Oregon State Police Detective Alan Corson and Multnomah County Sheriff's Detective John Ingram, who were in charge of the case, questioned Sosnovske and interviewed Pavlinac several times. Sosnovske, of course, denied everything, but despite really having had nothing to do with the crime, he failed two lie detector tests.

Corson and Ingram knew that something seemed off about the whole story, but eventually Pavlinac convinced them by bringing in the cut off button fly from a pair of jeans. Too bad the police didn't try to match it up to Bennett's ripped jeans because it wouldn't have fit—in fact, it was cut from Pavlinac's daughter's jeans. They then asked Pavlinac to show them where they had dumped the body, and through some calculated guessing and a little "luck," she only missed it by about 15 feet. Since it had been dark at the time, they figured that was close enough, and even though Pavlinac couldn't tell them where Bennett's purse or other belongings were, both Sosnovske and Pavlinac were charged with Bennett's murder.

Sosnovske, who had repeatedly claimed his innocence, was forced to plead guilty to avoid getting the death penalty. Pavlinac, who had also confessed her guilt, changed her story at the last minute and started saying that she was innocent after finding out that she faced life in prison, with no chance of parole for 10 years. But by then it was too late and nobody believed her, especially in light of her tape-recorded confessions, which had helped convict the pair. As the Bennett case was closed, Pavlinac and Sosnovske settled in to their new life behind bars in the Oregon State Penitentiary.

Meanwhile, Jesperson was looking for his next murder victim. Although it would be two and a half years before he killed again, his second murder almost took place just over three months after the first. On Thursday, April 12, 1990, as Jesperson was driving his Chevy through Shasta, California, on his way to Sacramento, he ran into 21-year-old mother Daun Slagle in a shopping mall parking lot. She had her four-month-old son with her and was visibly upset after having had a fight with her husband. Jesperson chatted with her for a while and then finally got Slagle to agree to go for a drive in the country with him, but she soon realized that it wasn't a very good idea. Jesperson sexually assaulted her and tried to force her to give him oral sex, but she resisted. Becoming angry, he pinned her up against the door with her face pressed to the window and tried to break her neck; terrified, she heard her neck snap several times and felt the strain as it was twisted.

During the violent struggle, her baby fell to the floor and started to cry. Suddenly, Jesperson relented and started the car, driving back into town and staring straight ahead the whole way; then he stopped and let Slagle out. She became Jesperson's only known living victim. When he arrived in Corning, California, Jesperson was arrested for the misdemeanor of sexual battery but not the felony of attempted murder. He pleaded no contest and was let go, which turned out to be a fatal mistake…for Jesperson's future victims.

In early August 1992, during a trucking run, Jesperson picked up a woman named Claudia at a brake-check spot near San Bernardino, California. He tied her up with duct tape, raped her and choked her several times, letting her pass out before reviving her—except for the last time. He called this a "death game" and would "play" it several more times with other victims. Afterwards, he dumped the body near Blythe, California, and covered it with tumbleweeds. The body was discovered a few weeks later, on August 30.

The next month, Jesperson killed Cynthia Lynn Rose at a truck stop near Turlock, California. She was his only victim that he didn't either rape or play the "death game" with; he simply resented the fact that she had let herself into his truck while he was sleeping. Apparently, she had been a prostitute looking for some action but wouldn't listen when Jesperson said he wasn't interested. When her body was found along the nearby highway, there were no signs of any foul play so her death was originally ruled a drug overdose.

In November 1992, Jesperson murdered another prostitute, 26-year-old Laurie Ann Pentland, in Salem, Oregon. He had picked her up at a truck stop in Wilsonville, and after they had sex, she tried to double the agreed-upon price. She taunted him by threatening to call the cops, so he strangled her and dropped her body off behind a G.I. Joe's store. Because of her fly-by-night lifestyle, police had no leads, and the investigation didn't last long.

Things settled down for over six months, until July 1993, when Jesperson killed a woman that the police described as a "street person." He had taken her to dinner in Corning, California, after offering to drive her to Sacramento, and then had raped her. He dumped her body by the side of the state highway west of Santa Nella, where it was found a few days later. Again, there were no signs of foul play and no leads, so she, too, was written off as a victim of a drug overdose.

Jesperson, who was either displeased that his murders were being written off as accidental or was having a crisis of conscience, started writing letters to the authorities and the media, claiming responsibility for killing Bennett and all the previously labeled Jane Does—including Claudia and the "street person." One letter was mailed to the courthouse in Clark County, Washington, while another was sent to a columnist at *The Oregonian* newspaper. Jesperson's tone was boastful, and he detailed how he had thrown away Bennett's Walkman and stolen a couple of dollars from her purse, and then had cut the fly from her jeans. Jesperson signed all his letters with a roughly drawn happy face instead of his name, earning him the nickname the "Happy Face Killer." But in stark contrast to the traditionally uplifting symbol, the letter claimed, "I do not want to kill again, and I want to protect my family from grief. I would tear it apart."

Despite that claim, Jesperson almost let the whole thing slip while having breakfast at a truck stop with his 15-year-old daughter, Melissa, in August 1994.

"You know, Melissa, things aren't always what they seem to be," he said. "I have something to tell you, but you'll tell the police if I do."

Melissa felt sick over what she thought was coming, so she went to the bathroom to calm down. When she came back, Jesperson had changed the subject, and Melissa didn't want to bring it up again. If she had, and her father had revealed his secret, who knows what Melissa's fate would have been.

Meanwhile, the Happy Face letters were turned over to the police, but they didn't have enough evidence to figure out who wrote them. However, since he had mentioned the "street person" from Corning, that investigation was reopened.

A year after the Corning murder, Jasperson killed a 40-year-old woman named Susanne farther away from his home base than any of his other victims. Her body was found on September 14, 1994, beside Interstate 10 west of Crestview, Florida. By the time a road crew came across her, only bones remained, so even though they tried to do forensic facial reconstruction to identify her, once again the police had no luck.

In January 1995, Jesperson picked up 21-year-old Angela Subrize at a hotel bar near Spokane, Washington. This time, after spending the night together, Jesperson offered to take her to her father's place in Fort Collins, Colorado, and they rode together for about a week.

"I'd like to call my dad and let him know I'm coming," Subrize had said on the journey. "But I don't have a credit card to charge it to."

"No problem," Jesperson had told her. "You can use mine." So Subrize made the call and charged it to Jesperson's card, which turned out to be his brother's. But her father told her he didn't want to see her.

"I changed my mind," she told Jesperson. "Will you take me to Indiana instead? I'd like to see a friend there. My old boyfriend."

Jesperson started to get annoyed then, but became even more so when she kept bugging him as he tried to sleep at a truck stop near Cheyenne, Wyoming.

"Come on, Keith, let's go…I want to keep driving," she whined.

"You kidding me? Look out the window. It's pouring rain," he answered. "Anyway, I need a few hours sleep before I drive anymore."

"You call yourself a truck driver?" she pushed. "A good driver would keep going."

Jesperson reacted with rage, raping her and then choking her to death, before falling back to sleep. When he woke up, he tied her body under the truck and dragged it for over 10 miles so that her prints and face wouldn't be identifiable, then dumped the corpse beside Interstate 80 in Nebraska.

Her remains weren't found for another eight months, and then only with Jesperson's help.

In the meantime, Jesperson had met a woman he truly liked, and the couple got engaged. Her name was Julie Ann Winningham, a 41-year-old party girl from Camas, Washington, who had a drug addiction and a criminal record. But soon Jesperson decided that she was only after his money, and he got the impression that he was only funding her addiction. They argued about it a few times before Jesperson lost control. Whereas most people would have just broken up, he took the more permanent route and killed her instead, on March 10, 1995.

Her nude body was found dumped beside Highway 14 in Washougal, Washington. This time, police were able to identify her, so Detective Rick Buckner of the Clark County Sheriff's Department did some digging, contacting her friends and family. That's how Jesperson's name came up; he was described as a long-haul truck driver—a giant "Baby Huey type"—that Winningham had been spending a lot of time with and had recently gotten engaged to. Winningham had been living in Utah after splitting from her previous husband, who was also a truck driver. She had hooked up with Jesperson at a truck stop, and he had brought her back to Washington in February.

Buckner investigated Jesperson, but found no criminal record. In fact, the only public record in his name was his Yakima County divorce certificate from 1990. Then Buckner tracked down the trucking company that Jesperson was working for and got his current itinerary. It showed that Jesperson had headed out to Pennsylvania the day after Winningham's death. On his return trip, he was scheduled to go through Texas, New Mexico and Arizona; more specifically, Jesperson would be picking up a load at a fairground in the Las Cruces, New Mexico, on March 22.

Buckner went to Las Cruces to meet Jesperson, taking another detective with him and enlisting several local deputies just in case. When Jesperson arrived for his fairground pickup, he was picked up by the cops instead.

Back at the Las Cruces police department, Jesperson knew they were looking for a confession, but he wouldn't cooperate. They questioned him for six hours about Winningham's death, but he refused to answer anything.

"Are you going to answer my questions, or do you want an attorney to be present?" Buckner asked.

"I'd like an attorney," Jesperson replied.

"Why do you need one? Did you do something wrong?" Buckner pushed.

But the ploy didn't work, and eventually, with no concrete evidence, Buckner had to let him go. Jesperson agreed to let the police take blood and hair samples, as well as photos and fingerprints, and then was on his way. As Buckner went back to Washington, Jesperson headed to Arizona.

That night, Jesperson kept reliving what he had done in his mind. He was feeling tortured inside and tried to come up with some reasonable explanation as to why he had killed eight women. When he couldn't make sense of it, Jesperson tried to even the score by killing himself. He attempted to overdose on sleeping pills but just ended up throwing them up. He tried the same thing the next night with the same result.

On March 24, Jesperson decided to confess, either to relieve his guilty conscience or to get himself some leniency with the law—or a combination of both. First, he wrote a letter to his brother, Brad, that said: "Seems like my luck has run out. I will never be able to enjoy life on the outside again. I got into a bad situation and got caught up with emotion. I killed a woman in my truck during an argument…I am sorry that I turned out this way. I have been a killer for five years and have killed eight people, assaulted more. I guess I haven't learned anything." He went on to say that he had been taking his anger out on different people, all the while hoping he would be caught.

To make sure he wouldn't renege on his decision, Jesperson called Buckner from an Arizona restaurant and admitted to killing Winningham. Buckner told him to stay where he was and sent some local deputies to get him. Jesperson later said he was glad that, regardless of whether he ended up in prison or was executed, he wouldn't be able to kill anymore.

Almost a week later, on March 30, Buckner took Jesperson into custody and flew him back to Washington to be formally charged with Winningham's murder. When they got there, Jesperson called his brother and asked him to destroy the letter of confession, but Brad turned it over to the police instead. Buckner now knew that Jesperson had killed eight people, and he sent a memo to police stations across the country, asking if they had any unsolved homicides that might match up with the places where Jesperson had driven. He got 16 replies, some from neighboring states and some from much farther away.

The Jesperson investigation focused on female victims found near truck stops and along highways, and one such Oregon case looked like it might be a Jesperson job. A woman had disappeared from a truck stop near Wilsonville—the same area where Jesperson had picked up Laurie Ann Pentland—in August 1994, and her body had been found along the highway near Medford the next March, just after Jesperson's arrest. Unsolved cases in Utah and Nevada also seemed to have his stamp on them, but there still wasn't enough evidence to link him to any of the murders.

Luckily, Jesperson was about to help the investigators out. Like many killers who get put away for one of their crimes, he started bragging to his cellmates about what else he had done but hadn't been fingered for. It's like a twisted version of little kids playing in the sandbox, saying things like, "My truck's better than your truck," or "My dad's bigger than your dad." And, as with many criminals who spill the beans to their fellow inmates, another prisoner turned Jesperson in.

His lawyer, Thomas Phelan, advised Jesperson to keep quiet about his crimes, and had Keith followed the proffered advice, justice may never have been served—Jesperson would have been charged for one murder, and one murder only: Winningham's. Nobody would have known he was a serial killer or just how dangerous he could be, and his violent roadside killing spree might have continued.

But, of course, there was also Jesperson's incriminating letter to Brad. Phelan asked him about the letter, and it didn't take long for Jesperson to let loose, spewing his deepest, darkest secrets as quickly as he could.

The first murder Jesperson claimed responsibility for was Angela Subrize's. In September 1995, he gave authorities specific directions as to where they would find her body. A few days later, a Nebraska highway patrolman located her decayed remains along Interstate 80 near the South Platte River, exactly where Jesperson had said they would be.

However, since it looked as though the murder had taken place in Wyoming, the investigation started there. Sergeant Terry Bohlig of the Laramie County Sheriff's Department discovered that Subrize had never been reported missing, since her family never knew where she was going to be next. Bohlig found Subrize's father by checking the calls charged to Jesperson's brother's credit card that Subrize had used that fateful day.

Wyoming authorities showed Jesperson a picture of Subrize, and he confirmed that she was the girl he had picked up and killed. They were sure they had their culprit as soon as Jesperson described the tattoo on Subrize's ankle: the cartoon character Tweety Bird making a rude gesture. Amazingly, the tattoo had remained intact even after Jesperson's attempt to remove all identifying features by dragging Subrize's body under his truck.

Now that Jesperson had admitted to killing Subrize in Wyoming, and even though the body had been dumped in Nebraska, he found himself in a legal bind he hadn't anticipated. Wyoming investigators were building a case so they could ask for the death penalty, and although Phelan tried to make a deal in which Jesperson would trade information on the murders in exchange for the right to live, Wyoming prosecutors rejected it.

Meanwhile, investigators in Washington, Oregon and California were examining Jesperson's handwriting, trying to figure out if he was the notorious Happy Face Killer. They compared the letter he had written to his brother to those sent to *The Oregonian*. The Happy Face letters claimed that he had killed three women in California and two in Oregon, and Jesperson's letter to Brad supported this claim by saying he had killed eight people in total. The Happy Face letters also gave further details about Claudia being bound with duct tape, a detail that had never been made public.

However, one of the Happy Face letters claimed that he had quit long-haul trucking to take another driving gig that put him more in the public spotlight, so he wouldn't be able to kill again, and Jesperson had clearly not done that.

During this time, Jesperson wrote another Happy Face letter from jail and had it smuggled out to *The Columbian* newspaper in Vancouver, Washington. In it, he said: "I know what I've done has been wrong, and I feel sorry for all the families of my victims. I am in fact the Happy Face Killer. I created that man because I wanted to be stopped, but it is hard to just come out and say it. I have prayed many nights in this cold, dark prison cell for the answer, and God has told me to come clear with it all, tell the truth about everything. I will not be happy until I am replacing that man in the Oregon State Penitentiary for the crime I did, and he goes free. Most people will say that I am a monster! I am not a monster! Just like the movie *Jurassic Park*, I was created by people."

This latest letter showed Jesperson trying to turn the tables and depict himself as a victim "created by people." It also showed remorse and a desire for justice, but it's unclear whether it was truly heartfelt or just an attempt to get a sweet deal. Right after this letter was received, which included reference to Sosnovske and Pavlinac being wrongly imprisoned for Bennett's murder—shocking investigators, who had been absolutely sure that Bennett's murder case had been properly solved—Jesperson's attorney asked the State of Oregon for a plea bargain.

But first there was some convincing to do and some evidence was required. Who was going to give a plea bargain to someone who previously had nothing to do with a crime? So Jesperson was taken on a closely guarded day trip, where he showed police the exact place where he had dumped Bennett's body almost six years earlier and where he had flung her purse—something that Pavlinac had never been able to do. Jesperson and Pavlinac were also given lie detector tests, and both were found to be telling the truth: Jesperson admitted that he killed Bennett, and Pavlinac insisted that she hadn't. So the process to release Pavlinac and Sosnovske began.

After his admissions, investigators from the Green River Killer Task Force visited Jesperson to see if he might be responsible for any of their unsolved murders. After all, Jesperson had done a lot of trucking in the area in the early to mid-'80s while he was hauling scrap metal to Seattle and Tacoma steel mills. But Jesperson quickly made up a tall tale to throw them off—he said that he had been driving up the Sea-Tac Strip one day when he accidentally ran over a hooker who had dodged out in front of his truck. When he went to a field to bury the body, he met another man who was also burying a body. Amazed at this coincidence, Jesperson introduced himself, and the two of them went to a restaurant to have coffee together. While discussing how alike the two victims had looked, Jesperson pulled out a necklace that he had taken off his. The other man got really emotional as they realized that they had each killed one of a set of identical twins.

While this story showed Jesperson's ability to lie on the fly, no sisters had ever been victims of the Green River killer.

Later, Jesperson admitted to concocting the story, but then again he claimed that his murder confessions were lies, too. So even though the Green River Task Force lost interest in him, it's hard not to wonder if maybe Jesperson actually was responsible for some of those murders. After all, they had very similar circumstances: mostly prostitutes or transient women who were strangled to death and left in outdoor locations, partially or totally nude.

These confessions and retractions weren't the only flip-flopping Jesperson did. At one point, while giving out details about all his murders, he claimed to have committed 166 of them. Nobody believed him, so he later retracted his statement.

He also waffled back and forth between showing remorse for his crimes and calling his victims "piles of garbage." That's how Jesperson referred to them on a website that he convinced a friend to create while still in prison. The website hyped a "Self-Start Serial Killer Kit" for sale. Some of the phony sales copy included: "Get rid of that unwanted family member! Get that job you always wanted by opening up the slot! Everyone will be dying to meet you!" It was a sick joke that made light of his murders, and finally, in 1997 AOL removed the website from their system at public request.

What was Jesperson's reasoning behind all of this? "I enjoy screwing with the press and prosecutors," he once told a reporter. "I do what has to be done to get results." And part of what he was trying to achieve was to avoid the death penalty.

In October 1995, instead of going to trial as scheduled, Jesperson pleaded guilty to the murder of Julie Ann Winningham. Clark County Superior Court Judge Robert L.

Harris gave him life imprisonment, but it wasn't that simple. The sentencing was delayed until two months later.

First, Jesperson was sent to Oregon to face new charges in Taunja Bennett's murder. On November 2, 1995, he pleaded no contest, and Multnomah County Presiding Judge Donald H. Londer sentenced him to life in prison with no eligibility for parole for 30 years. In a twisted way, this was exactly what Jesperson had wanted: prison time in Oregon, where he was safe from the death penalty, because if any other jurisdictions wanted to try him on his other murders, he would have to be extradited—a costly process involving a lot of bureaucratic red tape. He had waived his right to be extradited from Washington in order to get to Oregon in the first place.

In addition, the plea of "no contest" meant that other states would be less likely to enforce the death penalty later on, and it also meant that the process to release Pavlinac and Sosnovske could begin.

But there was still another Oregon murder case to deal with—that of Laurie Ann Pentland. After finding out that Jesperson was the Happy Face Killer, investigators used DNA analysis to link him to the crime. In his Happy Face letters, Jesperson had detailed his relationship with Pentland, saying she was an acquaintance that he had contacted on his CB radio while in Salem and had met for sex several times. Jesperson also confessed to her murder in his letters.

Because of this, Jesperson received another sentence of life in prison with no chance of parole for 30 years. After receiving his third life sentence, he was transferred to the Oregon State Penitentiary to serve two consecutive sentences…and if he's still alive when those are over, he'll head to the Washington State Penitentiary to start serving his next life sentence there.

On November 27, 1995, Laverne Pavlinac and John Sosnovske were released from prison after more than four years of doing time for a crime they didn't commit. Jesperson reportedly cried when he heard about it, perhaps out of happiness or maybe out of regret. If not for his own confession, after all, he never would have been caught.

Over two years later, and after lots of haggling, the State of Wyoming finally got Jesperson extradited for trial in Angela Subrize's murder. As prosecutors got ready for the trial during the next few months, Jesperson kept taunting authorities. He repeatedly changed his story about where exactly Subrize was killed, sometimes saying Wyoming, but other times claiming Nebraska. He threatened to keep deliberately misleading and confusing authorities about who had the right to prosecute him, thereby forcing a very expensive trial, unless they gave in to his demands. Finally they worked out a deal: Jesperson would plead guilty to murdering Subrize in Wyoming if Laramie County prosecutors took the death penalty off the table.

On June 3, 1998, District Judge Nicholas Kalokathis gave Jesperson his fourth consecutive life sentence, to be served in Wyoming when he was done in Oregon and Washington. That pretty well sealed Jesperson's fate—death penalty or not, he would eventually die in prison. He was then sent back to the Oregon State Penitentiary to continue serving his first sentence, and at the time of writing, Jesperson was still there.

But while he's out of sight, Jesperson's not necessarily out of mind. He's since made news headlines for starting a serial killer pen pal club and for selling his artwork, signed with a happy face, from behind bars.

Most recently, Jesperson's daughter, Melissa G. Moore, has been spotlighted by the media as she wrestles with the reality of having a serial killer for a father. Only a high school sophomore when Jesperson was sentenced to life in prison, Moore appeared on *Dr. Phil* and *The Oprah Winfrey Show* leading up to the release of her book *Shattered Silence* in September 2009. In the book, she shares her true story of trying to reconcile the father she thought she knew with the serial killer he truly was, and her slow realization that she couldn't have changed him; all she can do is control is her own life by deciding how to move on. Melissa's hope is that her story will inspire others to face their own challenges with optimism.

CHAPTER FIVE

Clarence Dayton Hillman
The Real Estate Manipulator
(1870–1935)

Crime and bad lives are the measure of a State's failure; all crime in the end is the crime of the community.

—H. G. Wells (1866–1946), British-born American author

"I heard you wanted to buy my house for $20,000," 21-year old Clarence Dayton Hillman said to the businessman who had sat near him on the train. He had overheard the man's conversation while the train was passing the house, and while he didn't actually own it yet, he got off at the next stop, went back and knocked on the door.

"Tell you what, I'll give you $15,000 for your house," he offered the homeowner.

"You got yourself a deal!" was the reply. Now he just needed to find the businessman again and sell him the house for $20,000 so he could pay the homeowner $15,000 and pocket the other $5000. A fair commission, Hillman thought, as he headed out to track the man down.

"That's right, I do want to buy your house," answered the businessman. Hillman had just made his fastest and biggest buck ever and knew that real estate was his calling.

Hillman was born in 1870 on a farm near Birmingham, Michigan, and was an orphan before he turned 10—his father died when he was five years old and his mother when he was nine. He had only achieved a second-grade formal education, but the Hillman family was a family of workers, not scholars. Rather than continuing with school, Hillman and his brother sold newspapers in Chicago.

In 1891, the Hillman brothers headed to California to try and strike it rich, and that train ride was the fateful one on which the talkative businessman saw the house he wanted to buy. Their timing couldn't have been worse, because two years later, the nation headed into a financial depression known as the Panic of 1893. But in 1896, just as the economy was taking an upward turn again, Hillman moved to Seattle, this time displaying perfect timing. The next year, gold was discovered in the Klondike, and Seattle was headed for boom times.

In the meantime, Hillman had been busy. He had platted, or mapped out, a subdivision around Green Lake, which at the time was well north of Seattle. Hillman's scheme was to buy cheap, logged-off land, which had very little agricultural value, and to divide it up into lots. Afterwards, while promoting the property, he made outrageous claims about the land's fertility, or its suitability for vacation resorts or industrial sites. He would take potential buyers on special excursions to show them the land, and sometimes they'd fight over it, driving the price up. Often it only took a few hours to sell his developments…and it was all thanks to a little false advertising.

A typical Hillman Land Company ad had slogans like: "All rich black soil, no better land on Earth," "Wheat twice the height of a man," "Strawberries the size of teacups," or "A fresh Jersey cow with every tract sold"—even though the low-grade land he was selling had probably never produced a crop worth getting excited about.

By 1902, Hillman had sold a total of 7000 lots in various subdivisions in and around Seattle, including Hillman's Schoolhouse Division, Green Lake Division, Lake Front Division, Kilbourne Division, South Shore Addition, Evan's Addition, Stinson's Addition and Woodland Park Division. Outside the city, he laid out Hillman City in Ranier Valley, as well as Hillman's Mountlake Terrace and Kennydale, named for his wife, Bessie, whose maiden name was Kenny. Just the Green Lake project alone netted Hillman $300,000, and apparently that land was good enough for him, because he built a lavish home there for himself and his family—Bessie and his three kids.

By 1903, Hillman was considered one of Seattle's most prominent businessmen and visionaries. But anyone who knew how he operated behind the scenes wouldn't likely have called him that. Most of his customers were new arrivals to the Northwest, with lots of ambition but not a lot of money. The people of pre-World War I America were excited about boomtowns, and Seattle was in the midst of it all. It was a gateway to the Klondike Gold Rush in the Yukon and the more recent Nome gold strike in Alaska, as well as a hub for the lumber boom in the surrounding area of Puget Sound. All this potential wealth had new immigrants fired up, and they were perhaps not as cautious as they might normally have been, making them gullible targets for a guy like Hillman. Some of them even bought lots from him through mail order, sight unseen.

Hillman took advantage of these people with stars—or, rather, gold—in their eyes and exploited the get-rich-quick mood of the times. He really wasn't a visionary so much as a good manipulator, a showman and, in most cases, a fraud. Even though P.T. Barnum never actually said, "There's a sucker born every minute," it's a phrase that's often attributed to him. But if there was anyone who should have coined that phrase, it was C.D. Hillman. Sometimes he sold the same lot to more than one person, and other times, he moved the boundary stakes after a sale had been completed. Some of the lots he sold were located at the bottom of Green Lake. And besides his fantastic claims about finding 12-foot-high wheat fields—something he always seemed shocked about when he was told that farmers failed to get that kind of crop from his land—he also promised, however falsely, that the Great Northern Railway Company was planning to build new train stations nearby.

"The American Dream is to own a home," he'd say, when questioned about the morality of his tactics. "I'm rendering all assistance possible to deserving people of limited means, to enable them to secure and pay for a home of their own."

It is often said that during the gold rush days, the people who were selling the tools to mine for gold made more than those buying the tools to mine the gold. Hillman took things to the next level and sold places for people to live before and after their trips to mine for gold. The difference was that the people selling tools were actually selling things that did what they were supposed to do—whereas Hillman was doing the equivalent of selling one pick to several different people, then feigning innocence when the pick that fell apart as soon as it hit the dirt.

But what would make a respected businessperson want to risk damaging his reputation by defrauding people? Sure, his schemes were based on greed and disrespect for other people, but you would think that, since Hillman was planning to stick around the Seattle area, he might have been more careful about ripping people off. And besides, some of his land was legitimately valuable, so it wouldn't have been too hard to play by the rules of decent society: don't tell outrageous lies, even in the name of marketing; make sure what you sell can be used for the purpose it's being sold for, without having to drain a lake to get at it; and only sell one thing to one person, not the same thing to many.

But apparently Hillman's racket was just too easy to pull off, seeing as the demand was much higher than the supply. He didn't have to bother putting in the effort to do things right or focus on quality and satisfied customers—people were literally throwing their money at him.

What's more interesting is the fact that locals didn't seem to see what was under Hillman's sheep's clothing. All business frauds must masquerade as legitimate entrepreneurs at some point—the extent of their façade depends on how good they are at covering up their scams. Strangely enough, despite doing things that should have been relatively easy to catch, Hillman continued operating in his underhanded way year after year.

By 1906, Hillman was still going strong. His newest developments included Pacific City, Auburndale and Jovita Heights. In April, Hillman purchased some land in the Green River Valley, between Seattle and Tacoma, where there was potential for a right-of-way to be built for an interurban railway between the two cities. Early descriptions of the land from homesteaders stated that it was full of "tall trees and lots of bears." Nonetheless, the peaty earth was rich and would be good for growing vegetation, so Hillman platted the area into lots that were 40 feet by 200 feet. The town was initially named Valley City, but in 1907, when they applied for a post office, they were told the town had to be renamed since there was already a Valley City in eastern Washington. The name they submitted was Algoma, which is a Native American word meaning "valley of flowers," but a typo gave the city the name Algona instead.

Durrell R. McAbee, who later became mayor of Algona, once commented on the city's unique layout. "There are two reasons for it," he said, "the nearby railroads and C.D. Hillman's garden tracts shell games." Many out-of-towners who arrived in Algona and adjoining Pacific City found that other families were already living on the rich "garden plots" they had just purchased.

Another of Hillman's schemes was Boston Harbor—formerly known as Dofflemyer Point—in Olympia, Washington—where, in 1907, he claimed to be building a thriving seaport that would put Boston, Massachusetts, to shame. Part of his marketing campaign involved advertising circulars that he sent out by mail. The pamphlets showed the Boston Harbor area as an impressive, well-developed city full of shipyards, mills, beautiful homes and happy, smiling people.

Thousands of Seattle residents were keen to see this thriving new development, so Hillman gave them a "free ride"—literally, if not figuratively—and took them in on a big paddleboat. One trip had 1700 people onboard the steamer *Yosemite*…and that only because that was as many as the ship would hold. More than 500 people were left standing at the dock, knowing they had missed the boat—both literally *and* figuratively. Before the steamer had even pulled in to Boston Harbor, Hillman had made an estimated $100,000 in sales.

But soon afterwards, people started noticing that Hillman had not only subdivided the land, but had also platted the bottom of the harbor into 30-foot by 100-foot plots. One of these unusable plots was sold a head-shaking 17 times.

Presumably Hillman must have been able to write these incidents off as honest mistakes, and luckily not every one of them made headlines. But on March 19, 1910, the *Auburn Argus* newspaper printed a story with the heading "Algona News." The article reported that Mr. and Mrs. John Hankins from Puyallup had come to Algona to see their newly acquired property on Eighth Avenue, which they had purchased from C.D. Hillman. When they arrived, however, they found the property nicely fenced, with a large two-story house already built…and the house was occupied by the Brown family. Since the Hankins held a valid warranty deed, and the Browns had a contract saying that all their payments were up to date, it quickly became obvious to all involved that Hillman must have sold the land twice. According to the story, both claimants were heading to Seattle that week to have Hillman make an adjustment.

Finally, Hillman ran his most elaborate scheme to date—the one that finally led to his downfall. In Port Susan, north of Everett in Snohomish County, he purchased 4000 acres of logged-off land, as well as the Port Susan Logging Railroad. He hid the slash that the loggers had left behind by planting large, pesky weeds like elephant grass and Himalayan blackberries. Then he did what had worked so well for Boston Harbor and started offering free trips to Port Susan for interested buyers.

On June 12, 1910, Hillman ran ads in the three largest Seattle newspapers, offering a "Grand Free Excursion" to what he called the New City of Birmingham. The price for the lots ranged from $65 to $150 per acre, and each lot was hyped as including beaches, lakes filled with fish and free transportation to move in.

He also got a steam organ, hung banners on it advertising the New City of Birmingham, and then hired a team of horses to pull it through the streets of Seattle. This time Hillman was advertising not only for buyers, but for salesmen. His criteria? Unbelievably, his sales force would apparently only include "honest, reliable men."

On June 14, 1910, Pier 6 at the foot of University Street was crowded with eager people trying to get a seat on the steamer *Venus* as part of their "Grand Free Excursion." A brass band entertained them on the trip, and they even got a free picnic lunch. As soon as the ship left the dock, Hillman started pitching to them.

"Birmingham is the place where rail meets sail," Hillman told his captive audience.

When the ship got to Birmingham, the potential buyers were greeted by an impressive layout: three large docks, a boardwalk that extended for two miles along the beach and a large sign welcoming them. The town already had two general stores, a department store, a sawmill, a church and a school. The Birmingham Railroad—with the former logging locomotive that Hillman had purchased—took interested passengers to see the other areas of the development that were farther out.

"The sun shines here in Birmingham 276 days a year," Hillman announced. "And the fruit orchards are abundant," he continued, offering everyone a taste from baskets of fresh fruit he had on hand as proof.

As you might've expected, it turned out that the fruit came from the Pike Place Market in Seattle. In fact, there were no orchards in Birmingham—nor were there were any businesses. The stores were totally fake and staffed by actors who were hired for the occasion. Furthermore, the sawmill didn't actually work—it was just a bunch of machinery piled together and not even connected properly. And no, the sun also didn't shine as much as he claimed—this *was* coastal Washington State, after all.

But nonetheless, 5000 five-acre tracts were sold within the first 60 days.

This time, however, wronged buyers fought back after finding out they had been tricked. Feeling they had been misled, some of them sued the *Seattle Star*—one of the papers that had run Hillman's ads—for libel. U.S. District Attorney Elmer E. Todd started tracking Hillman and his activities, and it ended up being Hillman's love of marketing by mail that sealed his fate. Mail fraud, after all, was a federal offense.

On September 21, 1910, two deputy U.S. marshalls and a postal inspector went to Hillman's offices in Seattle with a subpoena for the company books. The main offices housed the accounting ledgers for several of Hillman's Washington corporations: the Hillman Investment Company, the Boston Harbor Steamship & Land Company and the C.D. Hillman Snohomish County Railroad & Land Company. But since Hillman wasn't in his office that day, his bookkeeper, Edward D. Manning, was subpoenaed instead and brusquely

ordered to show up in Tacoma the very next m/
appear before the federal grand jury.

Since the books detailed everything from land deals,
expenditures and employment records back to September 1,
1907, and since Manning resented the police intrusion, he
refused to cooperate. The officers then seized the books, as
well as many other incriminating documents and papers.
Hillman's attorneys later contested the unorthodox seizure,
saying that the books were wrongfully produced for the
grand jury.

But in October 1910, Hillman was indicted on 13 counts
of using the U.S. postal system to defraud American citizens.
Following his trial, which started in January 1911, the jury
convicted Hillman on all counts, and he was sentenced to
two and a half years in prison on each count, to be served
concurrently. He was also fined $400 for each count, plus the
cost of the trial, for a total of $5200. In addition, he was given
a sentence of 20 days in the county jail for sending circulars
to prospective jurors, which put him in contempt of court.

Just prior to sentencing, Judge George Dunworth told
him, "Not only have you personally wronged poor people,
but you have maintained a corrupt organization that has
been a force of evil in the community."

But in light of all that, Hillman only ended up paying
a very small penance; a few years in prison and a few thousand dollars in fines was just a drop in the bucket when you
consider that Hillman had amassed a fortune of an estimated
seven million dollars.

Of course, Hillman appealed his conviction all the way to
the U.S. Supreme Court, but they refused to hear the case, so
his conviction and sentence were upheld in 1912.

While Hillman served a paltry 18 months at McNeil Island Penitentiary, his family stayed in the lush Hotel Del Coronado in San Diego and waited for his release in luxury. When he got out, Hillman kept his house in Seattle but redirected his real estate development ventures southward into California, where he continued to sell property in San Diego, Paso Robles and Pasadena.

In 1929, Hillman sent an offer to George S. Long, general manager of the Weyerhaeuser Timber Company, asking him if he'd like to buy thousands of acres of prime timberland located in five different Oregon counties. His letter stated, "We have owned this land for 15 years. We are leaving very shortly for a three-year trip around the world, so please make us your best offer." Long, however, turned Hillman down.

Bessie tried filing for divorce from Hillman three times while they were living in California, but they stayed married nonetheless. Hillman finally died in 1935 at the age of 65 while visiting his Paso Robles ranch, and he was buried in Seattle's Lake View Cemetery. His remains were supposed to be moved back to Paso Robles, where he had a plot waiting next to Bessie's, but his family never got around to it. His family also never put a proper headstone on his grave, so Seattle's biggest showman is no longer on show. That is, except for the Hillman name, which is still stamped on several cities, developments, and original land plats that are filed in numerous county land departments up and down the West Coast.

CHAPTER SIX

Ted Bundy
The Co-Ed Killer
(1946–89)

Murder is unique in that it abolishes the party it injures, so that society has to take the place of the victim and on his behalf demand atonement or grant forgiveness; it is the one crime in which society has a direct interest.

–W.H. Auden (1907–73), British-born American poet

The girl was sleeping soundly when Ted Bundy entered her room early in the morning on February 1, 1974. He knew that she had been out late having a few beers with her friends at Dante's, a popular hangout for university students, so she wouldn't wake up too easily. Lynda Ann Healy, 21 years old, lived with four other young women—one of whom was Bundy's cousin—but she was the one that he was after. Lynda Ann was pretty, with long, straight brown hair, and he liked the sound of her voice. He had always enjoyed listening to talk radio to escape into another world, and when Healy announced the weather and ski conditions for western Washington every morning, she always sounded friendly. She was also a psychology student at the University of Washington, like Bundy had been, but she had grown up in an upper-middle-class household, which he had only dreamed of.

Without making a sound that might alert Healy's room-mates, Bundy knocked her unconscious with a crowbar, then took off her nightgown and hung it in the closet. Next, he dressed her in jeans and a T-shirt, wrapped her in the top bedsheet, remade her bed and carried her limp body out the unlocked door. Later, he would kill her and dispose of her body on Taylor Mountain, east of Issaquah—right in the area she used to read weather reports for. Healy became the first known victim of soon-to-be notorious serial killer Ted Bundy, but she was far from the last.

Bundy was born Theodore Robert Cowell on November 24, 1946, to Eleanor Louise Cowell. The 22-year-old department store clerk was unmarried, so Ted was brought into the world at the Elizabeth Lund Home for Unwed Mothers in Burlington, Vermont. Bundy's supposed father—either Lloyd Marshall or Jack Worthington, depending on who told the story—was an air force veteran who wanted nothing to do with his son. To make matters worse, Ted's birth certificate listed his father as "unknown," and later speculation by the family was that Eleanor's father, a violent and possibly deranged nurseryman named Samuel Cowell, was probably Ted's father.

If that was the case, then it went well with the charade; since Eleanor was the eldest of three girls, Ted was introduced into the Cowell household in Philadelphia as their brother instead of their nephew, as the son of what were actually his grandparents. Eleanor's parents were afraid that their daughter would be publicly chastised for having had a child out of wedlock, so they concocted the story to protect her. Some say it wasn't until Bundy was 21 and checking his birth records while visiting Vermont, that he finally learned that his "sister" was really his mother.

In 1950, when Ted was four, he and Eleanor moved to Tacoma, Washington, to live with uncle Jack Cowell and his family. Once there, she legally changed both her and her son's name—she started going by Louise Cowell, and he became Theodore Robert Nelson.

Uncle Jack was a music professor at the College of Puget Sound in Tacoma, and he was successful, cultivated and refined. While Ted hated Washington at first, thinking that the mill town of Puget Sound seemed too raw and ugly, he was immediately drawn to Jack and tried to model himself after him. Ted would forever afterwards reject anything he saw as being too "common" and lust after what he considered to be the "cultured" side of life. Whenever he didn't get it, he felt life had wronged him.

In May 1951, Louise married Johnnie Culpepper Bundy, a soft-spoken man from North Carolina with a southern drawl who worked as a cook at a Veterans Administration hospital south of Tacoma. Ted's name underwent its final alteration, becoming Theodore Robert Bundy. However, Ted never bonded with Johnnie and still considered himself a Cowell. The rift between them was so great that people often remembered Johnnie getting mad at Ted and yelling at him, something that was very out of character for him.

In the summer of 1951, Louise had a miscarriage, but the next year, a daughter, Linda, was born. She was followed by three more half-siblings for Bundy: Glenn in 1954, Sandra in 1956 and Richard in 1961. During these years, Ted spent a lot of time looking after his younger siblings, but he didn't enjoy it very much; he was embarrassed by his family's modest lifestyle and jealous of his cousin John, who was Jack's son.

In 1955, when Ted was nine years old, the Bundy family moved into a new neighborhood that Ted hated, but nonetheless he made fast friends with two boys who live nearby. Terry Storwick and Warren Dodge thought Ted was a little aloof, but he was also great company and they would remain close to Bundy throughout high school.

Ted's aloofness may have actually been because he was painfully shy. For his whole life, he never saw himself as being very attractive, even though some women described him as "beautiful." As a young child, he was mercilessly teased and bullied, and he preferred to be on his own. He would often disappear into the woods for hours with his collie, Lassie, or listen to late-night talk radio in his room, pretending to be part of a secret world in which the callers were really talking to him.

In high school, Ted was never invited to parties, didn't have any girlfriends and had no clue what his friends were talking about when they described what happened on dates. While his buddies started moving on into different social circles, he was being left behind. Suddenly he felt like he couldn't figure out what constituted "proper" social behavior. Before, he had been smart and funny, but now he started to withdraw more and more. Although Ted was developing physically into a handsome and athletic teenager, his maturity level was stunted.

Bundy took it hard when he tried out for baseball and basketball but didn't make the team, and he decided he must be too skinny to compete with the bigger boys. Bitter about the rejection, he turned to solo sports like skiing and started dabbling in crime to make it happen. Since ski equipment was expensive, Bundy stole it. Taking the example of a few other boys, he also started counterfeiting ski passes. He was never caught for these misdemeanors, and at the time, friends of the family would have been shocked to learn of his indiscretions—they thought of Ted as an honest churchgoer looking forward to a career in law enforcement.

Meanwhile, Bundy discovered that by speaking up in class, he commanded more respect from the other students. He was fairly articulate and hid his shyness by creating an image of himself as a serious scholar. In his senior year, his public-speaking skills helped the re-election efforts of a local Republican congressman, and he decided that he loved politics—it let him be assertive, confident and made him feel accepted—but it would be a few years yet before he got involved again.

Bundy graduated from Tacoma's Woodrow Wilson High School in 1965 and started attending the University of Puget Sound on a scholarship. For two semesters, while still living at home, he did well and was liked by his professors. But he was lonelier than before with his childhood friends no longer around, and he felt intimidated by the frat boys on campus. He refused to join a fraternity because he felt socially inept and wasn't sure how to relate to the self-assured members. He tried once more to put up a confident front in class as he had in high school, but the large lecture halls left him feeling like an anonymous nobody.

He bought a '58 Volkswagen Beetle for $400, which allowed him to escape university life whenever he wanted and drive off by himself. He loved VW Bugs and would own several of them during his lifetime.

After attending a lecture discussing the geography and culture of mainland China, Bundy decided that, besides being exotic and glamorous, China was a subject of study in which people might notice him more. So he transferred to the University of Washington in Seattle to take their top-ranked Asian Studies program. He got a dorm room, again rejecting the frat houses, and excelled in his schoolwork. He continued to build his image as a witty, scholarly and serious student who was becoming a handsome ladies' man to boot.

In 1967, Bundy met a beautiful student whose pseud-onyms included Stephanie Brooks and Marjorie Russell. She was close to six feet tall, with long, straight hair, but she had more than good looks going for her—she was also confident, wealthy and sophisticated. They hit it off right away, and Bundy fell head over heels in love for the first time in his life. He was slow to get involved sexually, since he didn't want to reveal his inexperience right away, but he did reveal his immaturity, often playing childish pranks on her that annoyed her, acting like a 12-year-old boy with a crush on a classmate.

In the summer of 1967, Bundy transferred to Stanford University in Palo Alto, California, to take an intensive Chinese-language program. He was trying to impress Stephanie but found himself thinking that he couldn't measure up to her success. He missed his routines and familiar surroundings, so he lost the usual confidence he had always had in the classroom and, as a result, his grades went downhill.

At this point, Stephanie had had enough; shortly after graduating from the University of Washington, she abruptly ended her relationship with Bundy. She later said that she wasn't ready to commit to him because he was too fawning and immature, and she didn't feel like he had any ambition or goals for the future.

Bundy was devastated over the breakup and couldn't concentrate on anything, so his grades suffered even more. For the autumn session, he went back to the University of Washington, applying to the architecture program instead because Stephanie had once admired an architect character in a movie. However, when he wasn't accepted into the architecture program, he took urban planning, but failed at that, too, and was forced to drop out of college by Christmas.

While traveling around the country in 1968, trying to get his life back on track, Bundy visited his birth town in Vermont and was dealt a second big blow—he found out that he was an illegitimate child, and that his "parents" were actually his grandparents.

That spring, he returned to Seattle and found jobs as a busboy and a grocery store night stocker. He also became friends with a thief and drug dealer named Richard, who encouraged him to shoplift and burglarize homes. Bundy stole things because he felt he deserved them and was excited by the danger. Experts on the behavior of serial killers say that this type of thrill-seeking, paired with the tendency to steal with a sense of entitlement rather than guilt, is common among psychopaths.

Around that time, Bundy bumped into an old high school acquaintance who was working, along with some of his other former classmates, for Art Fletcher, a city councilman striving to become the Republican nominee for lieutenant-governor. Bundy was asked if he might want to help out, too, and he jumped at the chance. He felt like he instantly belonged somewhere and suddenly had a social life again. He quit both his jobs and became a full-time political volunteer. While most people of his age with a political conscience were part of the peace movement, Bundy was at the opposite end of the spectrum, working for the establishment. He didn't want to associate with outcasts or poor people; he'd rather rub elbows with the affluent and influential.

Bundy became Fletcher's official driver for a while, but after the November election in which Fletcher came in second, there was no more work for Ted. However, he had been watching his politically connected colleagues very closely, and by now had perfected his façade of being a socially gifted and impeccably dressed intellectual. Bundy took a sales job in a Seattle department store that he had once shoplifted from and quickly discovered that he had the skills and the flair to sell women anything.

After saving up some money, Bundy sold his '58 Bug and headed to Philadelphia to see his grandfather. For the early months of 1969, he attended Temple University, taking theater arts and discovering that a little bit of makeup, a false mustache or a hat could dramatically change his appearance, making him mostly unrecognizable if he wanted to be.

He returned to Seattle in the summer of 1969 and stayed in a University District rooming house, where his landlady, Frieda Rogers, found him to be a gentle young man. One day, while drinking coffee together in the kitchen, Mrs. Rogers was about to swat a fly when Bundy yelled, "Don't kill it!" and let the fly out the window instead. How ironic that a man who literally wouldn't hurt a fly would soon become a notorious serial killer.

On September 30, 1969, Bundy went around the corner to the Sandpiper tavern, a college hangout where he liked to pick up girls. There he saw 24-year-old Elizabeth Kloepfer from across the room and was immediately attracted to her; she was a medical secretary and recent divorcee out on the town with some friends. Liz would later write a book called *Phantom Prince: My Life with Ted Bundy* under the pseudonym Elizabeth Kendall, though she has also been referred to as Meg Anders.

After downing a pitcher of beer, Bundy got up the courage to approach Liz and ask her to dance, but she told him she couldn't. While often that would have caused him to withdraw and become upset, this time the beer gave him courage, and he asked one of her friends instead, who eagerly said yes.

A few minutes later, Liz was on the dance floor after all, so Ted confidently smiled at her and said, "You're right, you really can't dance!"

Liz was hooked; she thought Bundy was charming and took him home with her that night. Both drunk, and fully clothed, they crashed in her bed. She thought she was sleeping with a law student working on a book about Vietnam, since that's how Bundy had introduced himself.

The next morning, Liz's young daughter, Joanie (not her real name) woke them up. Bundy took an instant liking to the little girl and found that he was really fond of Liz, too—he felt like he'd known her his whole life. Within three months, they were spending hours chatting on the phone, making love several nights a week, taking Joanie on trips, visiting Bundy's family and even talking marriage...until the day he dramatically ripped up the marriage license, claiming that it was too soon. Liz, however, was so in love that she easily forgave him. Meanwhile, when they weren't together, Bundy would hang around the university, peeping in windows and watching violent porn alone in his dorm room.

When Liz found out that Ted was still a couple of years away from graduating, she gave him some money towards his tuition, so he re-enrolled in the University of Washington for the 1970 school year. He chose psychology as his new major, because he thought it would be a good way to figure things out about himself, and he certainly wasn't the first or last psychology student to do so. He ended up doing very well in his studies, writing a paper on schizophrenia that earned him a lot of praise from his professor.

But still, Bundy kept committing petty thefts. He had a night job driving a delivery truck for a medical supply company called Ped-Line. Not only did he steal things from the doctors' offices he delivered to, but also from his bosses—the most noteworthy item being a container of plaster of Paris, used to make casts.

Bundy later started volunteering one night a week at the Seattle Crisis Clinic, manning the suicide hotline as part of a work-study program in conjunction with his psychology classes. One of his co-workers was former policewoman and aspiring true crime writer Ann Rule, who would later pen the number one best-selling book *The Stranger Beside Me: Ted Bundy—The Shocking Inside Story*. Their job at the hotline was to talk to desperate people who called in looking for help, and if they'd already attempted to take their lives, to keep them on the line until the call was traced and cops could reach them. Bundy found that he had a special gift for comforting women who were depressed over losing their husbands or boyfriends.

In 1972, Bundy graduated with a degree in psychology but decided that he'd rather become a lawyer. However, despite his good grades, he kept flunking the Law School Aptitude Test (LSAT).

In May, Bundy left his position at the crisis clinic and was hired through a federal grant to counsel psychiatric out-patients from the Harborview Hospital in Seattle. He was still seeing Liz, but had a brief affair with a fellow counselor, often referred to as Cynthia Holt. Holt later said that instead of offering guidance and support, Bundy had a tendency to lecture his cases. The hospital staff also suspected him of calling patients at home, threatening them anonymously and talking dirty to them.

He often felt that the patients represented a mirror of his own personal life; this scared him and made him feel helpless. He decided that what he had learned in school couldn't cure people, and while he hadn't failed psychology, psychology had failed him. Suddenly it wasn't about who he could help anymore, including himself, but who he could hurt.

Holt chillingly recalled how Bundy used to shove his forearm against her throat while they were making love, something that could have easily killed her, and how he constantly annoyed her by making her drive him through the hills behind Lake Sammamish—a future burial place for some of his murder victims.

Bundy returned to politics for the 1972 election, campaigning as a volunteer for Republican governor Dan Evans. Suddenly Ted's social life veered upwards again; he not only flirted with the young women he worked with, who were enchanted by his good looks and manners, but impressed the guys with his intelligence and dedication.

Meanwhile, Liz was beginning to see the hidden dark side of Bundy. He once left a crowbar in her apartment and was known to carry a surgical glove in his pocket; when she found out he was also stealing, he threatened to kill her if she turned him in. He started wanting to get rougher in their sex life, and one time, when she agreed to be tied up with her pantyhose, Bundy already knew exactly where she kept them. However, Liz was too worried about losing Ted—to another woman, or to his Republican Party friends—to pay attention to these early warning signs.

After the election, Bundy applied to law school again and was finally accepted by the University of Utah College of Law for the fall of 1973. While he waited, he worked at the Seattle Crime Commission for a month, where he wrote articles for their newsletter and, ironically, helped with early studies on white-collar crime and rape prevention.

The first mention of Ted Bundy's name in the newspaper was a positive one. It came after he was out shopping with Liz and chased down a purse snatcher, holding him until the police arrived. The *Seattle Times* wrote about his heroic efforts, though it wasn't the first time Bundy had been commended by the police. The Seattle Police Department had praised his heroism years earlier, after he rescued his friend Terry's young niece, Wendy, from drowning. Some sources report that it was a three-year-old boy Bundy saved, but this may have actually been a separate incident altogether.

Bundy's new political friends then helped him get a job at the King County Office of Law and Justice Planning, where he studied the recurrence of certain crimes among those convicted of minor offenses. While scouring thousands of King County arrest records, he was intrigued to learn that the various jurisdictions didn't cross-reference their crimes, nor did they coordinate their investigation efforts very well.

In May 1973, Bundy went to Olympia to work for Ross Davis, the new head of the Washington Republican Central Committee. He was paid $1000 a month to help with research projects and looked up to Davis like a favorite uncle. That summer, he spent time with the Davis family and often played with their two small kids. They all thought he was a nice young man, though Davis did notice a pair of handcuffs one time in the trunk of Bundy's recently purchased '68 VW Bug.

Bundy also spent a lot of time with law student Marlin Vortman and his wife, Sheila, who had both worked with Bundy in the 1972 Evans campaign. Vortman convinced Bundy to follow in his footsteps and to study law at the University of Puget Sound (UPS), where he could make local connections rather than going out of state.

Bundy chose to exclude Liz from this part of his life, as well as from his decision to go to San Francisco to look up Stephanie in July 1973. He hadn't stopped thinking about her over the years and wanted to show her the new and improved Ted: suave, debonair, mature and successful. This time, Stephanie was very impressed by what she saw and wanted more.

Back home for the fall semester, as he started law school at UPS, Bundy was miserable. The College of Law was in a temporary downtown office instead of in the Ivy League school he had envisioned, and he saw it as depressingly demeaning. Unable to get over how reality didn't match his vision, his schoolwork suffered, and he started flunking out. In December, Bundy had to reapply to Utah and was reaccepted, but not until the fall of 1974.

Over Christmas, Liz went to Utah to visit her family, while Stephanie came to Washington to visit Bundy. Not knowing about Liz, Stephanie started talking marriage with Ted, and Bundy let her think they were engaged. After seeing Stephanie off at the airport, Bundy drove over to see Liz, who was cooking in the kitchen—the perfect image of domestic bliss. Soon, they were passionately making love. Thinking that if he just ignored Stephanie, the awkward situation with her would disappear, Bundy didn't bother to call his supposed fiancée anymore.

On January 4, 1974, Bundy committed his first crime in a series of rapes and murders that has been estimated as low as 36 victims, but could be as high as 100. The reason for the discrepancy is that Bundy was very good at hiding the bodies —almost as good as he was at hiding his true thoughts and emotions—and they usually weren't found until there was little left to identify them or the cause of death. Some experts have even speculated that Bundy's murderous tendencies could have started as far back as 1961; when he was 14 years old, an eight-year-old girl named Ann Marie Burr disappeared from her Tacoma home, though Bundy always denied killing her. Several times on death row, he also hinted that his first attempt at kidnapping was in 1969, and his first murder was in 1972.

Either way, Joni Lentz (a pseudonym) was the first known and confirmed victim, and one of only a few survivors. Shortly after midnight that morning, Bundy sneaked into the basement of the large Seattle house that the 18-year-old dancer and University of Washington student shared with several roommates. While she slept, he broke a rod off the frame of her bed, bashed her over the head, then sexually assaulted her with it. When she didn't come down for breakfast that morning, nobody suspected a thing, but later that day, her roommates got concerned and went to check on her. She looked to be asleep, but it turned out she was comatose and lying in a pool of blood. Her horrified roommates frantically called the police and the paramedics, and luckily Joni, after being in a coma for the next 10 days, miraculously survived the attack.

Almost a month later, after getting out of a class at UPS in Tacoma, Bundy attacked and later killed Lynda Ann Healy in Seattle. When she didn't show up for work at the radio station the next morning or for dinner at her parents' that night, the search was on. As Healy's disappearance was making headlines in Seattle's papers, Bundy talked to Stephanie for the last time. For the past seven years, he had thought about her. It was the classic story of boy meets girl, boy loses girl, boy wins girl back—but this time it was also boy dumps girl. She had hurt him, and now he wanted to hurt her.

On that Saturday evening, while Bundy was drinking beer, she called him at his apartment. "Why haven't you written or called?" she yelled into the phone. "How can you treat me like this?"

Bundy just listened without reacting while she continued on. "Don't you ever get in touch with me again," she warned him.

"Alright, far out," Bundy replied nonchalantly, hanging up and cracking open another can of beer. He might've said that he felt relieved that Stephanie was gone, but there was much more to the story than that. Over the next several months, female college students started disappearing at a rate of about one per month, all at the hands of Ted Bundy. When looking back at his first victims, several striking similarities become obvious: the women were all young, white, pretty, tall and slender, with long, brown hair. In other words, they all bore a striking physical resemblance to Stephanie, Bundy's first girlfriend, whom he apparently hadn't gotten over after all. Could his killing spree have been a twisted attempt to torture his ex-girlfriend and to hurt her more than she had hurt him?

On March 12, 1974, Bundy abducted and murdered 19-year-old Donna Gail Manson, a student at The Evergreen State College in Olympia, as she left her dorm room to go to a jazz concert. On April 17, he put his arm in a sling and went to the Central Washington State College campus in Ellensburg, where he approached several students and asked if they would help him carry a load of books to his Volkswagen. Susan Rancourt, who had just left a meeting with her dorm advisers, was kind-hearted enough to help— and lost her life because of it. On May 6, Bundy filled his gas tank and headed south on a 500-mile round trip, stopping long enough to abduct Kathy Parks from the Oregon State University campus in Corvallis, Oregon.

Then Bundy found a summer job at the Washington State Department Emergency Services (DES) in Olympia. Morbidly, part of the agency's duties included searching for Healy, Manson and Rancourt.

One of the women at the DES who fell under Bundy's charming spell was its best employee, Carole Boone. One day, Boone would become Bundy's wife and the mother of his child, but for now, they just flirted and became close friends.

On June 1, Brenda Ball—the first Bundy victim who wasn't a college student—disappeared after leaving The Flame Tavern in Burien, Washington. Ten days later, on June 11, he approached Georgeann Hawkins on the University of Washington campus, this time wearing a fake cast on his leg and asking for help carrying a briefcase to his VW Bug. She had been heading home from her boyfriend's dorm room to her Kappa Alpha Theta sorority house when she agreed to give him a hand, and she was never seen again.

Bundy finished his Washington murder rampage on July 14, 1974, by putting the sling on his arm and approaching women in Issaquah's Lake Sammamish State Park. He introduced himself to each of them as Ted and spoke with a fake British accent as he asked if they would help him unload a sailboat from his Volkswagen. One potential victim agreed and went with him to his car, but backed off and ran away when she saw that there was no sailboat. Unfortunately, Janice Ott didn't notice in time to escape; she left the beach to give him a hand and was kidnapped and killed by Bundy. Four hours later, Denise Naslund suffered the same fate. An hour after that, Bundy was at Liz's doorstep wanting dinner because he was starving.

King County detectives started distributing flyers through-out Seattle describing the suspect and his car, and included a composite sketch based on eyewitness recollections; the story was reported in both the local newspapers and television stations. Boone and some other co-workers kidded Bundy about how much he resembled the "Ted" in the drawing, and several people who knew him called the tip line to report him as a suspect—including Liz, eventually, despite not wanting to believe it. However, seeing as the police were wading through 200 tips a day, a well-dressed, polite law student didn't register very prominently on their criminal radar.

On September 2, after bidding Liz goodbye and driving off towards Salt Lake City to attend the University of Utah as planned, Bundy picked up a hitchhiker in Idaho, then raped and strangled her. A few days later, on September 7, the remains of Ott and Naslund were discovered, in pieces, off Interstate 90 near Issaquah, about a mile from where they disappeared. A few extra bones were also found, which belonged to Hawkins. It would be another six months—not until March 1, 1975—before bones from Healy, Rancourt, Parks and Ball were found on Taylor Mountain.

Bundy continued killing young women in Utah during October and November, including Melissa Smith, the 17-year-old daughter of Midvale Police Chief Louis Smith. He had often worried about his daughter's safety, and his worst fears came true on October 18 when Bundy raped, sodomized and strangled her.

But on November 8, a botched abduction turned the tables for Bundy. Posing as a policeman, he convinced 18-year-old Carol DaRonch to leave a mall and go with him to the parking lot to check on her car, where he claimed to have seen someone trying to break in. He then said she needed to accompany him back to the police station in his VW, but she was wary, so she didn't buckle her seat belt. When he stopped the car and tried to handcuff her, she struggled and broke free. Then he tried to hit her over the head with his crowbar, but she blocked the blow, kicked Bundy in the genitals and escaped. Frantically, she flagged down a passing car, and the couple inside took her to the police station for real, where she reported the crime.

In early 1975, Bundy started taking monthly trips to Colorado, murdering four more women between January and April, including 23-year-old Caryn Campbell. Then on May 6, he lured 12-year-old Lynette Culver away from her junior high school in Pocatello, Idaho, then raped and drowned her in his hotel room at the Holiday Inn.

In Washington, investigators had been narrowing down leads and had just moved Bundy's file to the "To Be Investigated" pile when Utah police notified them of his arrest. On August 16, 1975, Sergeant Bob Hayward had been patrolling a neighborhood he knew pretty well when he saw Bundy's tan Volkswagen Beetle and thought it looked suspicious. When he turned on his headlights to check the license plate, Bundy turned his off and drove away at high speed. Hayward chased him until Bundy finally pulled over at a gas station. A quick check of the trunk revealed a crowbar, ski mask, handcuffs and other tools, so Bundy was arrested on suspicion of burglary.

On October 2, 1975, Carol DaRonch and two witnesses from one of the Utah abductions picked Bundy out of a lineup. Over the next few weeks, other witnesses from Lake Sammamish also positively identified him.

Bundy's trial for the kidnapping of DaRonch began on February 23, 1976. He tried his best to be charming and was sure he'd be let off for lack of evidence, but the judge found him guilty of aggravated kidnapping and sentenced him to up to 15 years behind bars.

On October 22, Colorado police charged Bundy with Campbell's murder, and, in April 1977, he was extradited to Colorado to await a November trial. He said he wanted to defend himself, so he was given permission to use the courthouse library in Aspen. On June 7, when nobody was looking, he jumped out a second-story library window and escaped. Bundy laid low for about a week but was captured again while trying to leave town in a stolen car.

With a new January 1978 trial date and another jail transfer looming, Bundy escaped again on December 30, 1977, by crawling up through the ceiling and into the jailer's apartment, then walking out the front door. It was 15 hours before they even noticed he was gone, and by then, he was well on his way to Tallahassee, Florida, via Illinois, Michigan and Georgia. Using the name Chris Hagen, he rented an apartment near Florida State University.

After just two weeks of freedom, Bundy murdered again, this time attempting to massacre the entire Chi Omega sorority house on Saturday night, January 14, 1978. He violently attacked four sleeping students in their rooms, one at a time, by hitting them over the head with a club and knocking them unconscious. Two were killed—and Bundy bit one of them on the buttocks and nipple, leaving marks that later helped convict him—and two survived, but were severely injured and ended up crippled for life. A fellow sorority sister happened to come home just as Bundy ran out and was later able to identify him, but not before he attacked another young woman just a few blocks away.

Then on February 9, Bundy kidnapped and murdered 12-year-old Kimberly Leach. Almost a week later, Bundy's suspicious Volkswagen gave him away during another routine neighborhood watch. This time he had an orange Beetle, which Pensacola officer David Lee didn't recognize, so he ran a check on the plates and discovered the car had been reported stolen. Like the officer in Utah, he flashed him with his headlights, and again, Bundy tried to lose him, but with the same results—he was soon apprehended, and this time for good.

On July 31, 1978, Bundy was charged with the murder of Kimberly Leach, and afterwards with the Chi Omega sorority house murders. Almost a year later, on June 25, 1979, Bundy went to trial for the Chi Omega case and defended himself. A month later, the jury deliberated for seven hours before coming back with a verdict of guilty. Judge Cowart handed Bundy the death penalty for each of the two murders, to be delivered by the electric chair.

The Leach trial started January 7, 1980, in Orlando, Florida. This time Bundy employed two defense attorneys, who argued that he was not guilty by reason of insanity. However, a month later, history was repeated as the jury deliberated for seven hours again, and again returned the verdict of guilty.

The sentencing trial began on February 9, one year after Bundy had murdered Leach. With Carole Boone on the witness stand and Bundy interviewing her, the pair made jaws drop throughout the courtroom as they exchanged vows—a legal marriage since it was performed under oath. Immediately afterwards, Bundy got his wedding present: a third death sentence in the electric chair. He went back to death row for his honeymoon and stayed there almost nine years.

During that time, Bundy helped Dr. Bob Keppel, chief criminal investigator for the Washington State Attorney General, try to track down the Green River Killer, whose identity was not yet known. In the process, he not only suggested new ways to find the killer but gave officials a glimpse into his own criminal mind. Then just before his execution, Bundy confessed to several more crimes, describing them to Keppel in shocking detail.

The original execution date was set for March 4, 1986, but was postponed as Bundy went through several lengthy appeal processes. Finally, on January 24, 1989, at 7:00 AM, Bundy was executed. Outside, numerous news crews and hundreds of bystanders waited to hear that the deed had been done. After the official announcement of Bundy's death, the crowd cheered jubilantly and set off fireworks.

Eerily, the remains of one of the world's most notorious serial killers, Ted Bundy, will always be in Washington State, near the burial ground he used for several of his first victims. At his family's request, Bundy's body was cremated after his execution, and his ashes were spread over Washington's mountains.

CHAPTER SEVEN

Maxwell Levy
The Crimper King
(d. 1931)

Obviously crime pays, or there'd be no crime.

—G. Gordon Liddy (1930–), American politician

"Hey, Ed, I've got some men here that are ready to go on board that ship," he said to the Deputy U.S. Shipping Commissioner, who didn't even take a second look at the sailors. But Ed Sims did take a quick peek at the paperwork that his friend, Maxwell Levy, was holding in front of his face, before looking up at him with a twinkle in his eye.

"Five sailors altogether," Levy continued. "Do I have your approval on them?"

The men were slumped together in a rowboat just off shore, apparently sleeping in a half-sitting position, as another man sat on the seat with the oars in his hands. One of the sailors stirred and moaned, then flopped his head onto another's shoulder. Sims seemed to notice them for the first time, glancing at the rowboat from his spot on the wharf, but looked away quickly.

"Looks good to me," Sims answered, scribbling his signature on the paper that Levy held. "Send 'em on out to sea."

Levy smiled. "Thanks, Ed!" he called, as he went over to the ship's captain. "They're all yours, Captain!" Levy said, holding out his hand for the cash. The captain counted out $250—$50 for each of the men—and looked at Levy.

"And $40 each for the room and board at the New Sailor's Home," Levy said, as the captain gave him another $200.

"Much obliged, Captain—my men will row them out to your ship and help you get them onboard. Have a great trip!" Levy said cheerfully as he headed back to the New Sailor's Home, the boardinghouse he owned thanks to financial backing from Ed Sims.

Maxwell Levy had been living in the booming port town of Port Townsend, Washington, for about 15 years now, give or take a few depending on whether you counted his time prospecting in Alaska during the Klondike Gold Rush. He had arrived in the late 1880s from his birthplace of San Francisco and immediately settled in as a local businessman, partnering with Thomas Newman in the Chicago Clothing Company before becoming a saloon owner. Then he caught gold fever and headed up north to find his fortune. While in Alaska, he met and married his first wife, Harriet, but they divorced after returning to Port Townsend in 1899.

Soon after that, Levy married Lucy Hogg, the daughter of a local sea captain. He knew a lot of the local captains quite well because he worked with them on a regular basis. In a sense, his relationship with Lucy would continue, too, even though the marriage didn't last. In 1903, they had a son, James Maxwell Levy, but divorced shortly after he was born. Lucy then married another local businessman, Ed Sims, who also happened to be the deputy U.S. shipping commissioner.

Sims and Levy became friends, and when Levy asked Sims for financial backing so he could buy a share in the local sailor's boardinghouse and saloon, the New Sailor's Home, Sims agreed. The boardinghouse was on Water Street, near the wharf, so it was perfect for sailors who came ashore looking for a place to spend all the money they had earned at sea.

Of course, sailors who were feeling land under their feet for the first time in a long time really tended to go overboard with their celebrating. As a result, those who ran out of cash would have to rely on boardinghouse owners to cover their expenses until they got their next paying gig, and in Port Townsend, that man was Levy. He'd record the debts the sailors racked up at his establishment as an advance against the wages they'd receive when they headed back out to sea, and the ship's captain they worked for would repay Levy that money before paying the sailor. On top of that, captains paid Levy a finder's fee for each of the men he provided for their crews, which could be as much as $90 apiece, plus a clothing allowance of $20.

This arrangement meant that captains were paying good money for their crew, and that sailors who had done a lot of partying at the New Sailor's Home would often be working for little or no pay on their next trip. Obviously, that prospect didn't make them very enthusiastic to be heading back out to sea, but what could they do? They were indebted to both Levy, who gave them credit at the boardinghouse, and the ship's captain, who had paid off their debt.

Levy charged a premium price for this credit-based offer, and often, these drunken sailors didn't realize that their bills at the New Sailor's Home would end up being so high, so they'd try to back out of the deal. But Levy had other ways to get them on board the ships, even though most of them were illegal.

To "shanghai" someone means to make a sailor serve on a ship's crew against his wishes, either through force, coercion, kidnapping or by drugging him or getting him drunk. The term came about because sometimes a ship would be heading to the Far East, and a sailor would wake up on board to discover he'd been "sent to Shanghai." And for 20 years, Levy shanghaied sailors without ever being convicted of a crime. Someone who shanghais sailors is called a "crimper," and Levy was soon known as the "Crimper King."

During Levy's heyday, laws were in place to try to curb that sort of activity. A law was passed in 1895 that stated that sailors had to be fully aware of what they were doing when they signed up to be part of a ship's crew. That meant they couldn't be intoxicated, unconscious or asleep. To ensure that the law was followed, a consul of the country that owned the ship or a U.S. shipping commissioner had to witness each sailor's signature. Since Ed Sims, Levy's ex-wife's husband and his business partner and friend, had the power to validate a sailor's willingness and fitness to go aboard a ship, Levy's racket was allowed to run as a pretty well-oiled—and extremely lucrative—machine. But even before Sims came along, Levy had a very profitable crimping business.

There was rarely a shortage of customers on both sides of the coin—sailors who needed a place to stay overnight and ship's captains who were looking for a crew. Since the New Sailor's Home was a nice-looking, brick boardinghouse right on the waterfront, it attracted a lot of sailors as they came into port. And as those men left their ship, the captain needed to replace them, and he always knew he could count on Levy to supply enough sailors to fill his demand. As long as they were able-bodied men, why would the captain care how they came to be onboard his ship?

Usually, it wasn't Levy who did the actual shanghaiing. He was more the mastermind of the operation, running the show and giving orders to his henchmen, who were called "runners." These runners were given a quota of sailors to round up, and they didn't have second thoughts about using force to make it happen. Often they would just sit around the bar, waiting for a sailor to get drunk and pass out. If the man was good at holding his liquor, though, and it was taking too long for him to pass out, the runners would slip "knock-out drops" into his drink. Then they'd load him into a rowboat and take him out to a ship, which would be waiting in the harbor. By the time the sailor woke up, the ship was already well out into the ocean.

The term "sailor" was used loosely, too. Sometimes the shanghaied victims were professional boatmen, but if they couldn't find enough actual sailors, the runners were known to take soldiers, loggers, farmhands or even homeless people. Some of them were found playing a game of cards, and others were just hanging around the saloon. Their background or race didn't matter, with one exception: Native Americans were protected by the Bureau of Indian Affairs, so the federal government was sure to start investigating if there was ever a complaint involving a shanghaied Native. Levy didn't want to alert the feds to his scheme, so he told his runners not to pick up any Natives, or any local Port Townsend residents for that matter.

Although it might seem that Levy did this because he respected the members of his community, it was more about not getting caught. After all, if a local was shanghaied, he'd probably come back to town eventually, and that would just mean that Levy's neighbors would be mad at him—maybe exacting revenge or turning him in—rather than just some faceless strangers that he might never see again. Levy was motivated solely by cash and would do whatever it took to make the most money possible, which also meant continuing his scheme for as long as possible. There was never any regard or a second thought for the people he hurt along the way, as long as he profited from them.

Sometimes Levy was even able to get paid twice for the same crew by selling the men to one captain, and then convincing them to abandon ship by telling them that there were better working conditions on another ship. Then he'd resell the first crew to the second ship, which would be just like the first, or might even have worse conditions. Not only did Levy receive two payments for the same crew, but since the first ship still needed a crew, the captain paid him again to supply another crew. One time, he convinced three separate crews to abandon the *America* before it was actually able to leave, and he got paid for each one. In fact, except for the last crew that finally sailed with the *America*, Levy was paid twice for each crew.

Charles Gunderson was Levy's toughest and most notorious runner, and he often beat men senseless in order to shanghai them. One night Levy sent Gunderson and another runner, known as Chilean Pete, to sneak onto a British ship that was moored in the harbor and to pay the sailors to desert it. Levy had already been paid for the crew once and was planning to sell them to another ship for a second payment, as well as getting paid again to replenish the British ship.

But the British ship's mate and boatswain discovered the pair onboard before the deal was done and pursued Gunderson and Pete as they hightailed it to their skiff, rowing as fast as they could back to Levy's boardinghouse. As the British officers came up behind them in another rowboat, Gunderson swung an oar and tried to knock them out, so the ship's mate fired his gun at the runners. Chilean Pete was killed, and Gunderson was wounded by a bullet to the shoulder.

The ship's mate and Gunderson went to trial, where the jury acquitted both of them. The ship's mate was let off because Chilean Pete had been caught in the middle of an act of piracy; Gunderson wasn't convicted because he claimed that the sailors had invited him to visit the ship, and he hadn't even made it onboard.

But all of Levy's capers weren't just about shanghaiing men. Before buying into the New Sailor's Home with the help of Sims, Levy had owned another establishment known for attracting sailors; the Latona Saloon had been a regular hangout for non-union sailors in particular. Early in the evening on August 11, 1893, a non-union sailor who had been badly beaten up stumbled into the Latona Saloon, claiming he'd been attacked by union sailors. In fact, some of them had followed him there, and, as if on cue, a large, angry crowd of men was soon gathered across the street.

The non-union sailors in the bar taunted the union sailors outside and vice versa, until a union sailor tried to enter the saloon, and Levy stopped him. Gunderson and the bartender, Robert Kirk, were close behind, armed with weapons.

"You'd best be staying away, unless you're looking for trouble," Gunderson warned.

"Yeah? How are you gonna make us?" sneered the union sailor as his buddies swarmed in behind him, and they all pushed their way through the door.

At that point, all hell broke loose…shots were fired every which way and fists flew. One of the waiters, Otto Anderson, was injured by a stray bullet to the stomach, and a bystander, Ricordo Gueraro—who had just come by to see what all the noise was about—ended up getting shot in the leg. One union sailor, James Connor, was shot in the right hip and shoulder, and another, Joseph Dixon, cut his arm while smashing through one of the saloon's windows. Soon, every single window on the ground floor was broken, and the saloon looked as if it had just been hit by a hurricane.

Eventually, the police arrived and broke up the ruckus. The mob of union sailors wanted to lynch Levy, Gunderson and Kirk, so officer Brophy escorted the threesome to jail to keep them safe. Later, a bunch of union men tried to continue the fight and weren't arrested until the next night, when they were thrown into a cell on the other side of the jail.

The union men were charged with inciting a riot and destroying the Latona Saloon. Levy and his boys were charged with assault and went to trial, defended by attorney A.R. Coleman from the shipowner's association of San Francisco. Coleman argued that Levy and the men had been trying to defend themselves. He claimed that Gunderson had just fired warning shots into the floor, but the union sailors had ignored the gesture and attacked anyhow. Ralston and Lanstrum, a couple of the non-union sailors, supported the story. They testified that Levy had only come out from the bar, unarmed, to try to make peace and settle everyone down.

The union men were represented by attorneys James Hamilton Lewis and E.S. Lyons, who claimed that Levy had beaten and kicked the man who tried to enter the saloon, and had done it without any provocation at all. Union agents McGlynn and Benedikton testified that it hadn't even been a union issue; the man had simply lost his ring at the Latona Saloon a few weeks earlier and had just been going there to get it back. They said the fight didn't start until he had been kicked out of the bar by Levy.

In the end, two trials were necessary because the first one ended with a hung jury. The second jury eventually acquitted both Levy and the union men who had been charged with inciting the riot. But far from ending without consequences, the whole incident seems to have been instrumental in settling labor disputes that had caused the initial tension; shortly afterwards, the union agreed to a five-dollar-per-month pay cut for deep-sea-going vessels, as well as various other salary reductions.

It may have seemed that, throughout this episode, Levy was a friend to the underdog sailors, but after he was released from jail, he went right back to taking their money and shanghaiing them. And he often ran his schemes like he was a true mafia boss; once, when a ship's captain hired a sailor without Levy's consent, he and his runners beat them both up.

He also had a habit of cutting corners so he would earn a larger profit from each transaction. Even though the captains usually gave him extra money to pay for clothes and other necessities for each sailor, Levy sometimes skimped on what he provided and pocketed the rest. Once he supplied 20 sailors to a British ship, but they all threatened to mutiny before the ship had even left port. The captain called Levy, who brought in the British consul to help, but Levy wasn't the one the consul ended up helping. The consul spoke to each of the sailors about why they were upset and discovered that the clothing Levy had given the men was dirty, torn or smelling of garbage, and some of it was even women's clothing. The consul immediately ordered Levy to start supplying proper attire for the sailors and that was the last time he tried pulling that trick.

In early 1896, Levy shanghaied a couple of men for a British ship that was about to leave and had one of his runners, Thomas Newman, help him row them out to the ship. After leaving the men onboard and starting to row back, one of the shanghaied men tried to escape by jumping overboard. Newman rescued him from the water, but his thanks were short-lived because Levy then beat him up for trying to escape. Levy was charged with assault with a deadly weapon, but the case ended up being dismissed.

In May of the same year, Levy and Newman were charged with theft before U.S. Commissioner James G. Swan. A sailor named Alex Von Hagen claimed that they had stolen his baggage after Newman stored it onboard his ship, then refused to return it until Von Hagen signed a promissory note for $50, which was supposedly the amount of the bill he owed Levy for room and board. But Von Hagen said the bill was way too much for the time he had stayed at the New Sailor's Home.

Levy admitted to the commissioner that they had indeed taken Von Hagen's luggage, but said they would have given it back if anyone had asked for it. This case was dismissed, too, but Swan sent an assistant to accompany Levy and Von Hagen to where the bags were stored and to make sure they were properly returned.

Just a few days later, Levy was in trouble with the law again. He was seen approaching a sailor named Charles M. Carlson, who was leaning against the railing outside the Red Front Clothing House, and then throwing a rock at him. Carlson ended up with an injured eye, and Levy was charged with assault and battery.

A large crowd showed up hoping to see Levy convicted. M.B. Sachs defended him while the city attorney prosecuted the case. Carlson claimed the attack had been completely unprovoked, and three eyewitnesses, admitting they didn't know what may have happened to cause it, corroborated that Levy had thrown the rock at him. William Debbert, Eugene Thurlow and Charles Webber were standing in the street when they saw it happen, and they all said that they didn't see Carlson fight back.

Then Levy took the stand and said that Carlson had been hindering his boardinghouse business by trying to lure men away from him. "When I saw Carlson standing by the Red Front store, I just wanted to talk to him about what he was doing," he testified. "In the middle of the conversation, he kicked me in the stomach, and I was just defending myself when I hit him back."

Two other witnesses supported Levy's story by saying that they saw Carlson start the fight, but Webber and Debbert insisted that they didn't see Carlson kick Levy at all, and Carlson denied that he had. Because of the opposing stories, the jury couldn't decide on a verdict, and once again, the case was dismissed.

In January 1897, Levy sold a crew to the British ship *Chiltonford* and then planned to sell the men a second time later that night. He made a deal with the ship to have his employee, Adrian Sheehan, watch over the sailors while they were in the harbor, allegedly to protect them from other crimpers who might steal the crew. But Levy was the only person who planned to steal them; he had Sheehan get the sailors drunk so they would willingly go with him when Levy arrived later to sell them to another ship.

However, the ship's captain knew what Levy and Sheehan were up to and stood watch, ready and waiting for what was coming next. When Levy's men arrived, he fired his gun to scare them away, and the sailors stayed with the *Chiltonford.*

In 1899, Levy was asked to find a crew of 10 men for the *British General,* but since it was the height of the gold rush, there was a shortage of sailors in port. A lot of them had enlisted with ships sailing to Alaska, which was a gateway to the Yukon River gold fields in Canada. So Levy called his friend David Evans from Tacoma, who was able to round up five men, while Levy found the other five. But most of the men were farmers or other tradesmen, and only two of them had any sailing experience to speak of. However, since the ship's captain was under a tight deadline to sail, he didn't have time to be choosy and off they went. Luckily, despite sailing with a crew full of novices, the *British General* arrived at her destination safe and sound.

The story didn't end quite so happily for another man who Levy shanghaied and sent to Hong Kong on a ship. All he wanted was to get revenge on Levy, and he thought about it every day for the whole two years that he was away. When he finally made it back to Port Townsend, his first stop was Levy's office. He found Levy there talking to two of his runners, and three-against-one is bad odds at the best of times, especially when you were talking about Levy's men. But the shanghaied man was so angry and worked up that his sense of judgment must not have been working at full capacity. He attacked Levy's men by jumping on them, but he was soon lying unconscious on the ground.

Another time, Gunderson found himself the target of a shanghaied man's revenge scheme. It all started when Gunderson tried to get the man drunk, but he was one of those guys who could hold his liquor without passing out. So after a while, Gunderson just picked up a bar stool and swung it at him, knocking him to the ground and then kicking him in the face. Gunderson dragged the unconscious bloke to a ship that was headed for Australia and left him onboard. The shanghaied sailor came back to Port Townsend at his first opportunity, hunted Gunderson down and assaulted him with a knife. Gunderson was stabbed seven times in the neck and arms, and although he survived the attack, he suffered severe tendon damage. That was the final straw for Gunderson, who decided that he no longer wanted to be associated with a crook like Levy. Instead, he spent the rest of his life working as a fisherman.

Levy's days in the business were numbered, too. In fact, the whole shanghaiing racket stopped abruptly in 1906, when new laws were passed that prohibited any steamship agency, shipping professional or runner from hiring a drunken sailor. On top of that, any sailor onboard any ship could disembark with just cause if he brought his case before the board of commissioners. Those who didn't obey the new law faced steep fines of $200 to $500 every time it happened.

These new parameters made it very tough for Levy to continue business as usual. He tried to keep it going for a while, keeping a very low profile, but several other factors gave rise to the end of the shady practice. First, steamships started replacing sailing vessels, and these new ships didn't need such large crews. That meant less demand for Levy's potential supply of sailors, and eventually fewer customers wanted to stay in his boardinghouse. And the sailors that continued working found their rights more protected than ever, as unions got more involved.

By 1910, Levy had been dethroned and was no longer considered the Crimper King…or any type of crimper at all. In 1912, he and his family moved to San Francisco, where he lived in relative obscurity for almost 20 years until his death in 1931.

CHAPTER EIGHT

Linda Burfield Hazzard
The Starvation Doctor
(1867–1938)

Society prepares the crime, the criminal commits it.

–Henry Thomas Buckle (1821–62), English historian
and author

"I'd like to store your valuables for you, dear," the doctor said to the sickly woman lying in her bed. Claire Williamson struggled to prop herself up and look the fasting specialist in the face. Claire had become fond of this woman, who was in her eyes a gifted healer and a kind, motherly type.

"I could look after your things while you get well," Dr. Linda Burfield Hazzard continued. She wasn't actually a doctor, but everyone—well, almost everyone—called her that. "I have a safe in my office, and they'll be much better off there."

"I don't see how anyone could get into our apartments to steal anything," Dora Williamson replied, smiling reassuredly at her bedridden sister.

"I agree," Claire replied. "It seems that we are quite safe here. There's no need to worry."

"But it really would be better to put them in my care," Hazzard insisted. It was the third time she had made the suggestion, and Dora was on the verge of giving in.

"Well…I suppose it wouldn't hurt to have our valuables in a safe," she relented.

"And your rings, too," Hazzard said, smiling and taking Dora's hand to slip the diamond rings off her fingers. Then she continued, "What about your land deeds? Do you have any, dear?"

"Yes, I have deeds to some land in Vancouver," Dora replied.

"Alright, I can take those, too. I'll secure everything in my office safe for a few days, and then take it to the bank for you," said Hazzard, holding out her hand for the paperwork.

The Williamson sisters, for the most part, were pretty self-sufficient. That is, they were before they met Hazzard. In an effort to improve their health, they ended up destroying it by putting full trust in someone that others considered a quack.

Then again, they weren't the only ones; lots of competent people trusted Hazzard's "expertise" over the years. The Williamson sisters may have been some of Hazzard's most lucrative prey, but they certainly weren't her first—or her last.

Linda Burfield was born in 1867 in Carver County, Minnesota, to an American father and a Canadian and English mother. She married her first husband when she was 18, and they had two kids together, but in 1898, she left her family behind to become a career woman in Minneapolis. She had had some training as an osteopathic nurse when she was younger, but even though she wasn't qualified, Linda insisted on calling herself a doctor. Her medical philosophy was based on the theory that fasting could cure anything, no matter how big or small the malady, because the source of all disease was "impure blood" caused by "impaired digestion." Fasting allowed the digestive system to "rest," which was the body's "only means of recuperation," allowing it to be "cleansed of impurities." She also claimed to have studied with one of the other popular fasting advocates of the day, Dr. Edward Hooker Dewey, author of *The Gospel of Health*.

But Linda's methods took things a few steps further by including daily enemas that went on for hours a time and conducting what she called "osteopathic massage," which involved beating her fists violently against her patients' bodies, supposedly to help eliminate toxins.

She killed her first patient in Minneapolis in 1902, just as her divorce became final. The coroner tried to have her prosecuted after he discovered that her patient had starved to death, but Burfield couldn't be held accountable because, ironically, she wasn't licensed to practice medicine—an interesting loophole that she no doubt noted. Investigators asked Burfield what had happened to the victim's rings and other valuables, but she refused to answer.

Two years later, Linda married Sam Christman Hazzard, a graduate of the U.S. Military Academy at West Point who later destroyed his own career by misappropriating Army funds. Sam Hazzard was the definition of tall, dark and handsome—over six feet tall, with broad shoulders, black hair and a huge mustache. But he looked distressed and always smelled slightly of alcohol. He had been married twice before and was still married to someone else when he wed

Linda. After a high-profile bigamy trial, Sam was sentenced to two years in prison. When he was released in 1906, the couple moved to Washington State to start a new life, and Linda started "practicing" in Seattle, commuting from their 40-acre property in the Kitsap County town of Olalla. She called the property "Wilderness Heights" and planned to build a large sanitarium there someday.

Some of the more free-thinking and holistic-minded locals thought that Hazzard's medical theories were just what the doctor ordered, so to speak. After all, she was enough of an expert to have followed in her mentor's footsteps and had written a book of her own in 1908, entitled *Fasting for the Cure of Disease*. The beginning of her book read, "Appetite is Craving; Hunger is Desire. Craving is never satisfied, but Desire is relieved when Want is supplied. Eating without Hunger, or pandering to Appetite at the expense of Digestion, makes Disease inevitable."

And that wasn't Hazzard's only book over the years; she wrote more than 10 of them on the same topic, and since they're in the public domain and have since been republished, you can actually still buy, borrow or download nearly all of them today.

One of her fans was Daisey Maud Haglund, a Norwegian woman whose immigrant parents had previously owned Alki Point, the westernmost point in West Seattle. In 1908, just after her book was published, Hazzard put Haglund on a 50-day fast. She died on her birthday, February 8, leaving behind her three-year-old son, Ivar. Haglund was Hazzard's first recorded victim in Washington, and little Ivar, consciously or subconsciously, apparently didn't want to see anyone else starve—he grew up and became the owner of some very successful seafood restaurants in the Seattle area, including the still-popular Ivar's Acres of Clams, Ivar's Salmon House and Ivar's Seafood Bars. He also founded Ivar's brand clam chowder, which is enjoyed around the world to this day.

Later that year, on September 26, Hazzard starved Ida Wilcox to death; in 1909, it was Viola Heaton on March 24 and Blanche B. Tindall on June 18. Then 26-year-old Eugene Stanley Wakelin's decomposing remains were found on the Hazzards' property, shot in the head and presumed to be a victim of suicide. But it turned out that Linda Hazzard had power of attorney over Wakelin's estate—he had been the son of a British lord, and she had wired his lawyers to ask for more money to pay his mortuary bill. The British vice-consul in Tacoma later speculated that perhaps Wakelin had been shot by the Hazzards, who were upset to discover that he wasn't actually rich, despite his aristocratic background.

On July 20, 1910, Maude Whitney was killed, and on March 29, 1911, 24-year-old civil engineer Earl Edward Erdman became Hazzard's latest victim. Erdman died only three weeks after undertaking Hazzard's "cure." While he was waiting on the operating table for an emergency blood transfusion, the *Seattle Daily Times* ran a headline that said, "Woman 'M.D.' Kills Another Patient." The very next day, however, Hazzard was officially awarded her license to practice medicine in Washington. Even though she didn't have a medical degree, Hazzard was given the privilege along with 28 other alternative medicine practitioners. Hazzard then took to calling herself the only licensed fasting therapist in the country, which made her the top choice for what was beginning to be a very popular treatment.

Strangely, unbelievably, even when it became well publicized that people were dying while being treated by Hazzard,
patients kept coming to her—and some of them were very
intelligent people. Almost exactly two months after Erdman,
on May 30, Frank Southard died under Hazzard's care; he
had been a partner in the law firm of Morris, Southard and
Shipley. Then there was C.A. Harrison, who had been the
publisher of the *Alaska-Yukon* magazine, and Ivan Flux, an
Englishman who had come to America to purchase a ranch.
While Flux fasted for 53 days, Hazzard managed to get hold
of his money and property, and told his family that he had
died with only $70 to his name.

Authorities tried to intervene a few times, including when
Lewis Ellsworth Rader drastically began losing weight in
1911. He was a former legislator and publisher of *Sound
Views* magazine. While Hazzard was treating him at the
Outlook Hotel, health inspectors tried to convince him to
leave, but he refused, and Hazzard administered his treatments
in a secret location to avoid further interference. When Rader
died on May 11, he weighed less than one hundred pounds—
abnormally skinny for a man who was five-foot-eleven.

In nearly all the deaths besides Wakelin's, the autopsy
reports listed starvation as the cause of death—that is, unless
Hazzard performed the autopsy, in which case she'd always
list some other cause. Right in her book, she even writes, "It
is questionable whether, in a conscious being, death has ever
resulted from starvation, or, in other words, from the
exhaustion of body tissue as brain food. No evidence that
can be taken as conclusive shows this to be the fact."

Seattle's health director said he couldn't step in, because not
only was Hazzard licensed, but all her patients were willingly

taking her treatment. But the truth was that many of Hazzard's patients were afraid of her and her overbearing, larger-than-life personality and wouldn't dare disobey her orders. However, this was only the case for the patients who were already under Hazzard's care. You would think that all the repeated deaths and the horribly emaciated condition of the patients who passed away would be a big, red warning flag to potential patients, despite her official medical license.

Then again, it's possible that the disclaimer written in the introduction to her book is what convinced people to keep seeking her out for treatment:

> *Popular belief and medical teaching lead to the conclusion that abstinence from food for ten or twelve days will result in starvation and death. This is easily refuted. On my lists are considerably over one thousand instances of continuous fasts whose limits extend from ten to seventy-five days. While I esteem and consider but one cause and but one disease, the symptoms expressed in this long roll cover virtually the whole of medical pathology; and in twelve years only eleven patients have died while under my care. Each of these deaths has proved an occasion for persecution, malignment, prosecution, and injury; and from each and every case both I and the method have emerged triumphant, the autopsy showing organic disease, and that death was inevitable.*

Right…so even though fasting can allegedly cure any disease, since all disease has the same root cause, her patients didn't die of starvation while fasting; they died of the original disease that the fasting method was supposed to cure but couldn't. What a convenient excuse!

In theory, admittedly, the basis of her medical ideals may not have been totally wrong. In essence, Hazzard was advocating the treatment of the root cause of the disease, instead of just treating the symptoms. Her fasting regimen replaced the many drugs that conventional medicine typically prescribed, and most of her patients did feel better…if only at first.

In December 1905, 17-year-old Edward Anderson had been brought to see Hazzard, who was then still called Dr. Burfield while her husband was in prison for bigamy. His mother didn't believe in the fasting treatments, but it was her last resort; a medical doctor had said Edward was dying and there was no hope. He was being treated with everything from strychnine to codeine and had to be force-fed his meals. His body was swollen, and he couldn't move.

After just a few hours of being treated with a massage and enema, the boy said he was feeling better. After a few days on Hazzard's fast, his pain, fever and swelling stopped, and he was able to sleep properly. Then she introduced her tomato broth twice a day, increasing the amount as Edward got stronger. Hazzard claimed that within a month he was getting around on his own, and within six weeks, he was back at work, seemingly in perfect health.

Hazzard told this story again and again to lend credence to her methods. She also brought up the case of a 65-year-old woman named Mrs. J.B. Barnett from Kansas City, Missouri, who came to her office in Seattle with digestive issues that were causing melancholia and suicidal tendencies. After a 46-day fast, Barnett miraculously recovered, both physically and mentally. And then there was the 28-year-old housemaid

from Sweden, Amelia Larsen, who would have been committed to an asylum for violent tendencies if her sister
hadn't convinced her to undergo Hazzard's treatment. After
fasting for 43 days, Larsen went back to Sweden, happy,
healthy and completely sane.

Some of the other patients who said they felt better after
beginning the treatment were the Williamson sisters. Dorothea
Williamson, an original disbeliever, had to be convinced by her
sister, Claire, that they should both be treated by Hazzard;
she later admitted that the first few days of the fast made her
believe more strongly in Hazzard's methods than she ever
had before.

However, by the time they should have stopped believing
in the healing power of Hazzard's treatments, they were too
weak and delirious to notice or to do anything about it. To
them, it just confirmed how much they needed more treatments, especially since Hazzard told them it was perfectly
normal—she kept saying that this was the darkness before
the dawn, so to speak.

The Williamson sisters were rich British heiresses who
found out about Hazzard during a trip to Victoria, BC, when
they saw her ad in a Seattle newspaper. They were interested
in alternative medicine, and although they were only in their
early 30s and not what one might call unhealthy, they figured
they could become even more fit by undergoing some natural
remedies. They had the opportunity to travel the world and
buy whatever they liked thanks to their father, who had been
a wealthy English officer in the Imperial Army Medical
Service; but they felt that all their money hadn't allowed them
to buy health or happiness, so they were looking for a more
holistic solution.

They ordered a copy of Hazzard's book on September 2, 1910, and along with it, they received a brochure advertising her Institute of Natural Therapeutics in Olalla, Washington. Since the Williamsons had spent their fair share of time in sanitariums and health institutes during their travels, the concept wasn't anything new to them. In fact, it had become a bit of a hobby, even though their family didn't approve. Claire wrote back and forth to Hazzard a few times during the following months, mentioning her sister's health and exaggerating her slight digestive issues. Dorothea—who preferred to be called Dora—only went along with it because she adored her little sister and would have done anything for her. Sometimes it took some persuasion, but Dora nearly always ended up complying with what Claire wanted.

On February 27, 1911, at 11:00 AM, the Williamsons stood in Hazzard's office in the Northern Bank and Trust Building in Seattle. Brusquely shaking the girls' hands, Hazzard announced that they needed to begin treatment right away—without even examining them or asking them any health-related questions.

The sisters expressed their excitement about going to the sanitarium in Olalla, but Hazzard said it wasn't quite ready yet because rain had delayed construction. Instead, she started treating them right that minute by pummeling them on their backs and heads with her fists, administering her so-called osteopathic massage. She instructed them to return to her office for another treatment each weekday, in addition to the fasting and exercise she prescribed.

"Your bodies are full of poison," Hazzard told them. "You need to fast for three or four weeks, and you have to walk vigorously, several times a day, no matter how hard it is."

The Williamsons were only allowed to drink a broth made from boiled tomatoes, twice a day, and nothing else. Later, they were allowed to add asparagus to the broth and have a few tablespoons of orange juice. And they were given regular enemas—which Hazzard called "internal baths"— for hours at a time while the girls were curled up, knees to chest. Eventually, the enemas lasted all day, and when the patients became too weak to stay in the curled-up position, they were laid in canvas hammocks strung over the bathtub instead.

Hazzard assigned them to stay in a two-bedroom apartment at the Buena Vista, a nice apartment complex whose name meant "beautiful view," located in downtown Seattle on the corner of Boylston and Olive streets. She told them to let her know if anything about the accommodations was not to their liking—a consideration that convinced the sisters that Hazzard only wanted what was best for her patients.

Meanwhile, the Williamsons' family had no idea where Dora and Claire were; the women had lied and told everyone they were traveling in Canada on business, mainly because their relatives didn't approve of their penchant for seeking out alternative medical treatments. Unfortunately, that also made things much easier for Hazzard.

Despite frequent fainting spells, the sisters remained loyal to Hazzard. After all, even with her unorthodox ways, she seemed very knowledgeable, speaking with a voice of authority, and she was kindhearted to boot. They were absolutely sure that she really cared about them and their health.

"You'll feel weak after a certain point," she had explained to them, so they wouldn't be alarmed about their worsening condition. "But once the poison leaves your body, you'll be completely cured!"

Also attending to the Williamsons was Nellie Sherman, a nurse who had met Hazzard on a ferry trip and had started working for her despite having an already busy schedule. At first, she remained pretty hands off, but as the sisters got weaker and sicker, she tried to save them. First, she paid a visit to one of the other Buena Vista tenants, a busy, young, working woman named Clara Corrigan, who had seen the girls before and after being treated, had noticed their worsening condition and had offered Nellie any help she could give.

Then Nellie went behind Hazzard's back to see her friend in Seattle for advice, noted osteopath Dr. Augusta Brewer. Dr. Brewer, as it happened, had given Claire spinal treatments in July 1910, and said she didn't approve of Hazzard's methods. She knew Hazzard wasn't a doctor, refused to call her "Dr. Hazzard" and certainly wasn't about to rat out Nellie for dropping by and discussing Hazzard's "patients." She urged Nellie to try to give the girls the more food, stressing that Hazzard didn't know what she was doing. Unfortunately, Nellie knew very well that the sisters wouldn't take even a drop of water without Hazzard saying it was okay.

As the sisters wasted away, Hazzard told them that they mustn't discuss their finances with each other because they needed to focus on healing—and yet Hazzard kept pushing them to discuss it with her, telling them it must be difficult to take care of their affairs while in a strange country. Since the Williamsons were too weak to write, Hazzard had her attorney's secretary come by to take dictation, writing letters on the sisters' behalf.

"Does anyone in your family have authority over you?" Hazzard asked sweetly.

"No, we've been alone so long that we manage everything beautifully ourselves," Dora replied. That's when Hazzard started asking them to store their valuables in her safe.

As the fast continued, Claire lost the most weight, but Dora started to become mentally weak. She would ramble on, often confused and delirious.

"That's why doctors haven't been able to figure out what's wrong with you," Hazzard told her. "It's not your body that's the problem, but your brain."

In the early morning of April 21, 1911, Hazzard and Nellie packed up the Williamson sisters' belongings at the Buena Vista to take them to the Olalla sanitarium. They were loaded into ambulances, and several bystanders—including Clara, the owners of the Buena Vista and another tenant who had heard the Williamsons crying in pain for weeks—watched them go. Dora's hands and face were bound and covered with white bandages, and she looked ominously like a mummy. Claire looked to be less than 70 pounds, and Dora was just slightly heavier; no one expected to see them alive again.

As they lay in the ambulances, passing in and out of consciousness while waiting several hours to catch a special boat to Olalla, Hazzard's attorney, John Arthur, brought some paperwork for Claire to sign. It was an amendment to her will that left extra money to Hazzard and was addressed to Claire's longtime nursemaid and friend, Margaret Conway, in Australia. Margaret had cared for the girls during their childhood and had become like a mother to them when both their parents died. As adults, while the Williamsons traveled, they wrote regularly to Margaret—but they had never mentioned Seattle or Dr. Hazzard in any of their other letters.

Then Margaret received a mysterious telegram from Claire with a strange air of urgency, instructing Margaret to come see them in Seattle on a ship that was set to sail from Sydney on May 8. Claire must have managed to sneak that telegram out, but it was soon followed by a glowing letter about how amazing Dr. and Mr. Hazzard had been to them, and how healthy the sisters were becoming...except for Dora's brain, which Claire said might take a few more months to get better.

The new sanitarium in Olalla wasn't yet the glorious big structure that Hazzard envisioned; so far, it only consisted of their house and a few rickety cabins. Dora and Claire were kept in separate rooms of the Hazzard's home, and each one was told that her sister must not be disturbed. Dora was told that Claire was too weak to see anyone, and Claire was told that Dora was too demented. One time, when Dora used all her strength to crawl over and talk to her sister, the skeletal Claire instructed her to go back to her bed—as usual, Dora complied.

When Margaret arrived in Vancouver, BC, on June 1, Sam Hazzard was there to meet her. He told her that Dora was fine, but hopelessly insane...and that Claire had died. Margaret was dumbfounded. Dead? At 33 years old? But she had just finished reading the girl's last telegram, written only two weeks before, saying both sisters were "quite well!" The words were like a shot through the woman's heart, and she knew then that something was terribly, terribly wrong.

Margaret was taken to the morgue to see Claire, who was utterly unrecognizable. The girls' uncle from Portland, John Herbert, had also been at the sanitarium a few days before and was understandably upset that he hadn't been notified of Claire's illness before she died. Hazzard, who conducted the autopsy and embalming, said that she had died on May 19—just eight days after fellow patient Rader—of cirrhosis of the liver, caused by medication taken in childhood. In truth, right in front of Dora, Hazzard had given Claire one last punch to the stomach in the guise of a final osteopathic massage, and Claire had lost consciousness immediately afterwards. Then Hazzard had set Dora up in a bedroom with an open window, telling her repeatedly in a not-so-subliminal suggestion that she shouldn't try to kill herself by jumping out.

Herbert—otherwise known to the girls as Uncle Jack—was then presented with a typewritten, unsigned letter that Claire had supposedly dictated, saying that she and Dora had started treatment voluntarily, and if she died, it was meant to be. Before they went to Claire's funeral, he had been allowed to see Dora briefly, but was told that she couldn't take much excitement.

Margaret was also taken to Olalla to see Dora, who was now living alone in one of the roughly made cabins, a frail and ghastly blue pile of skin and bones. Dora begged Margaret to take her away but the next day insisted that she wanted to stay because the treatment was doing her so much good. Margaret knew better, though, and moved in with Dora to keep an eye on her. While taking over some nursing duties and pretending to follow Hazzard's regimen, Margaret started sneaking rice and flour into Dora's tomato broth, trying to build up her strength enough so they could leave.

On July 4, the few patients at Wilderness Heights were let out of their confined spaces for a celebration, and two of them secretly went to Margaret and begged her to help them escape their prison. This just confirmed Margaret's growing suspicions—she had already noticed that Hazzard was wearing Claire's favorite hat and silk dressing gown. She had also found out that Dora had been convinced to give Hazzard power of attorney, and they had already taken some of her money, which she had wanted to send to another uncle in Toronto. But that was just the tip of the iceberg in Hazzard's attempt to take control of the entire Williamson estate.

Tipped off to the true precariousness of Dora's health by Hazzard's former nurse, Sarah Robinson, Margaret started packing the Williamsons' trunks and told Hazzard that she was going to take Dora away. But an angry Hazzard said that, since she was now Dora's legal guardian, Dora would be staying at Wilderness Heights for the rest of her life—however long, or short, that might be.

"It was your dying sister's last wish," Hazzard explained to Dora, who had not consented to the guardianship; it had been granted by Kitsap County, at Hazzard's urging, after authorities had ruled Dora incompetent. "You wouldn't want to disappoint her—and you're so unbalanced that you couldn't possibly care for her yourself."

So Margaret sneaked off to cable Uncle Jack, who came over from Portland to rescue the now 60-pound Dora. Hazzard again brought up her appointed guardianship of Dora, but then relented. However, claiming that her lawyer had advised her to do so, she gave Uncle Jack a bill and said that she would let Dora leave if someone paid the balance owing on her $2000 statement. It was clearly extortion, Jack thought, but after a few hours of negotiation he got Hazzard to settle for a slightly smaller ransom. Then on July 22, a long 52 days after Margaret's arrival at the sanitarium, and close to 100 days for Dora, the trio finally left Olalla.

C.E. Lucien Agassiz, the British vice-consul in Tacoma, was outraged at the whole situation. He demanded that Kitsap County prosecute Hazzard, but they said it would be too expensive, so Dora offered to pay for it. In August 1911, Hazzard was arrested and a *Tacoma Daily News* headline read, "Officials Expect to Expose Starvation Atrocities: Dr. Hazzard Depicted as Fiend." News reports told the tales of the dead British heiress and of the virtual skeletons walking around the Hazzard house—now dubbed Starvation Heights.

Hazzard claimed she was being targeted for two reasons: she was a successful woman and traditional doctors were against natural cures. "I'm going to get on the stand and show up that bunch," she told reporters. "They've been playing checkers, but it's my move—I'll show them a thing or two!"

However, her lawyer didn't let her take the stand in her sensational three-week trial, and the judge also said that none of her former patients could, either. Hazzard was repri-manded several times for signaling to defense witnesses, which included loyal staff and the families of her patients, and trying to coach them on what to say. One of these was John Ivar Haglund, husband of Hazzard's first victim in Washington, who had continued taking little Ivar to see Hazzard three times a week. Another of her witnesses was accused of trying to bribe a nurse who had formerly worked at the sanitarium, and Agassiz's home was broken into midway through the trial, but only Claire's trunk of personal papers was looted—presumably by one of Hazzard's followers. There were a lot of them attending the trial; close to 250 women who were fans of Hazzard's came to the courthouse to lend her their support.

But the Williamsons' paper trail was the most convincing evidence, including Claire's changed will, several fake letters and telegrams, and a forged entry in her diary—replete with uncharacteristic misspellings and a reference to herself in the third person—saying that she wanted Hazzard to have her diamonds. "She's a serpent who trod sly and stealthy, yet with all her craft left a trail of slime," announced prosecuting attorney Thomas Stevenson. After being nursed back to health by Margaret, Dora also made a great prosecuting witness, as did photos of her just before she was rescued from Starvation Heights.

Throughout the trial, Hazzard was referred to as "Mrs. Hazzard," but she kept insisting, "It's Dr. Hazzard... Mrs. Hazzard is my mother-in-law." It didn't matter, though, because with or without her credentials or fancy titles, Hazzard lost the case. However, the jury delivered a final verdict of manslaughter rather than murder, which according to the *Town Crier* newspaper was probably only because she was female. While Hazzard waited to be sentenced, two more women and two babies died at her sanitarium.

On February 4, 1912, Hazzard was sentenced to two to 20 years of hard labor at the Washington State Penitentiary in Walla Walla, but she only ended up serving the minimum two years in prison. She was granted a pardon by the governor in exchange for leaving the country, so she went to New Zealand for a few years, but returned to Olalla in 1920 to pick up where she left off. While abroad, she had worked as a "physician," "dietician" and "osteopath," and had written another book, amassing enough money to finally build her dream sanitarium, a big, lavish building.

But the State of Washington had since revoked her medical license, so she called her new establishment a "school of health." Oddly for a school, it contained an autopsy room in the basement; a convenient amenity, considering that Hazzard continued to kill people through starvation—or whatever she was calling it.

Since Hazzard could have garnered the respect she thought she deserved by treating her patients to cleanses of reasonable lengths instead of these extreme and dangerous fasts, why did she insist on letting so many die? Was it simply greed and the fact that she had found a twisted loophole in the legal system that allowed her to take money from delirious patients who trusted her, just by convincing them to endorse her requests?

Some people theorized that Hazzard was putting a spell on all her patients, and, in a sense, she was very much like a cult leader—she prepared her patients for thought control through repetitive insistence that their bodies were full of poison and only she had the cure. She then severely decreased their nutrition intake and controlled their environment by keeping them locked up in a hotel suite or isolated cabin room on her property. She made it quite clear that punishment would come to those who left, not exactly through God, but in the form of their rebounding illness. Finally, her commanding personality and abrupt manner convinced everyone that she knew the absolute truth. Hazzard pulled it all off just as deftly as Franz Edmund Creffield had.

In 1935, the sanitarium burned to the ground—perhaps an accident, perhaps an act of revenge from someone she had harmed—and Hazzard only survived it by another three years. What was her cause of death, you ask? She started on one of her own fasting cures because she wasn't feeling well. Now that's poetic justice for you!

Considering that she treated herself even after her treatments had killed multiple patients, it is quite possible that Hazzard went to her grave thinking that she had done nothing wrong, that she had only tried to improve the health of those in her care. Or perhaps, like Creffield, she started out with some good intentions and eventually began to believe her own lies. But holding that belief would have meant she was as crazy and delirious as she made her patients. After all, those who do care don't steal from the people they're supposed to be treating—whether you're talking about money, health or freedom—and they don't put them in danger by pushing their treatment beyond what's safe. Obviously, they also don't kill people in the name of helping them get healthy.

Although Hazzard didn't fit the typical profile—the characteristics and experiences shared by Keith Hunter Jesperson, Ted Bundy and Gary Ridgway—she was definitely a serial killer in the strictest definition, and a fairly prolific one at that, with an estimated 40 victims.

In the end, Hazzard's name was very apt. She was a hazard to others as well as to herself.

CHAPTER NINE

Robert Stevenson
The Mount Scott Rapist
(1957–)

Rape is the only crime in which the victim becomes the accused.

—Freda Adler (1934–), American educator and author

"Who's there?" the woman gasped, propping herself up in bed and looking towards where the noise had come from. When she saw the shadowy figure with a knife in his hand hovering at the foot of her bed in the darkness, she screamed.

He quickly ran towards her, covering her mouth with his hand. "Don't scream!" he ordered. "I don't want to hurt you." He felt the pretty 27-year-old woman relax slightly under his grip. "If I take my hand away, are you going to scream again?" he asked cautiously.

Slowly but deliberately, she shook her head "no." Robert Wayne Stevenson, better known as the Mount Scott rapist, took his hand away, and the woman let loose the loudest scream she could muster.

Stevenson clamped his hand over her mouth again, this time pressing the cold knife against her throat. First, she struggled against him, trying to wriggle her way out of his arms. Then, with a small whimper and a sigh, she stopped moving, afraid that he'd slit her throat if she kept fighting.

Stevenson kept the knife against the woman's throat as he reached for a sock and stuffed it in her mouth. Then he tied her hands together and slowly undressed her. She stole a glance at the clock and saw that it was almost 3:00 AM on Wednesday, April 20, 1983. She had been asleep in her apartment in Mount Scott—a neighborhood in southeast Portland, Oregon—for only a few hours before this man had awoken her.

Now he was undressing himself, and she saw that he was already erect. Quickly and forcefully, he entered her. "Don't look at my face," he kept warning her. Over the next two and a half hours, he raped her four times. Once he tried to sodomize her but gave up when he couldn't do it easily.

After he was done, Stevenson untied his victim's hands, took the sock out of her mouth and put his knife on the floor beside the bed. Then he took a deep breath and, slumping forward, said, "Sometimes life just kind of sucks, you know?"

"Yeah," she answered quietly. "I know." She had similar feelings right now. How could this have happened to her? Why hadn't she checked the front door to make sure it was securely locked before she went to bed?

Then she realized that this was her chance to turn being a victim into a position of power, to gain the rapist's confidence and maybe learn something that could help the police convict him later.

"What is it that's been bothering you?" she asked tentatively.

Stevenson stole a glance at the girl. Maybe this was a good opportunity to ease his conscience by confessing his troubles to someone who wouldn't tell—she couldn't tell because he knew where she lived and how to get in. She'd be too afraid to open her mouth.

"You get married, and it's all supposed to be great. Then a couple of kids come along, and sometimes it just doesn't add up. There's something missing."

"Like what?" she asked.

"Oh, you know. Just like they say, the sex goes downhill. We've been having problems in that area for a while."

But Stevenson wasn't getting sexual satisfaction from the rapes, either. This girl was his third in three months—and then there had been two others that same month who he would have raped if they hadn't screamed so loudly before he had a chance to clamp their mouths shut and stuff socks in them. They, too, had left their doors unlocked, and he had gotten in okay, but even with the knife, he couldn't scare them enough to keep them quiet. Instead, he had been the one who had gotten scared and ran away.

The three girls he had raped, though, had all been good-looking, at least judging by what he could see in the dark, and had probably been close to his age of 25, he thought. But even so, Stevenson wasn't getting pleasure out of having sex with them. It was more like a power trip. He liked humiliating his victims and roughing them up.

Stevenson was born in June 1957. Like many people his age, he may have been feeling the pressure of being a quarter-century old and not living the life he had envisioned for himself. But most people don't react to the quarter-life crisis by doing what he did. They don't use force and violence to make others have sex, turning a normally intimate act into an extremely frightening experience. They don't steal people's innocence, completely disregarding the physical, mental and emotional impact it could have on them, both short term and long term. Was it a need to punish others in the bedroom, as he felt he was being punished? Or was it a desire to take what he felt he was owed?

The best that can be said about Stevenson is that he didn't kill anyone. And, as a token payback, he did feel some kind of remorse and maybe even suffered for it.

It had all started in the early morning hours of Tuesday, January 4, 1983. Stevenson had stayed in downtown Portland for several hours after getting off work Monday and had taken a late bus from the transit mall. A woman got on the bus, too, heading home after a busy night at her job. She was tired and was just looking forward to relaxing, so she didn't pay any attention to Stevenson, who was sitting a few rows behind her.

They both got off in Mount Scott; while she went out the front doors of the bus, feeling safe with the driver watching, Stevenson took the back exit. The woman pulled her coat collar up around her neck to shield herself from the cold winter air and walked quickly towards her home. As she went inside her apartment, he watched her from a distance…and then waited.

The woman took a bath and then fixed herself a late-night snack to eat in front of the TV. As she sat back and unwound to prepare for bed, she didn't give a second thought to whether or not she had locked the front door.

She lived alone, but Mount Scott was a good neighborhood, and her life was relatively peaceful.

She was so tired that she dozed off on the couch, and when she woke up, she noticed it was 1:30 AM. She turned off the TV and headed straight to bed, falling asleep even before her head hit the pillow. She didn't hear Stevenson when he slipped quietly through the door and sneaked into her bedroom. But she did hear him open and close one of her dresser drawers and take a step towards her bed. Within seconds, she was fully awake and sitting bolt upright, looking at the dark silhouette of a man at the foot of her bed. She opened her mouth and screamed.

Stevenson raced over, grabbing her hair with one hand and slapping his hand over her mouth with the other. "Don't scream, and I won't hurt you," he told her. "And don't look at my face."

She couldn't see his face very well in the dark, but she did see the gleam of a knife blade in the light from the streetlamp outside her window. She was scared, but she nodded her agreement that she wouldn't scream again. Stevenson put the knife under her chin, up against her throat, shoved a sock into her mouth and forced her to lie face down on the bed. Then he took a pair of her pantyhose and tied her hands behind her back with them.

After she was bound up, Stevenson tore off her underwear. She sobbed quietly while he stripped from the waist down, breathing heavily, and brutally entered her. She bit down on the sock in her mouth, waiting for it all to end as he robotically thrust against her body.

"Don't call the police," he ordered when he was finally finished. "I'll be watching you, and if you say anything, I'll know about it. I'll come back for you."

The frightened woman couldn't stop crying as he got dressed and left, not bothering to untie her or cover her up. Finally, she freed herself and, ignoring his threats, called 911.

"I've just been raped," she sobbed into the phone. "He attacked me in my bed and tied me up."

"Don't worry, ma'am, help is on its way," the dispatcher assured her. "Stay on the line, okay? I want you to speak with one of our specialists." The call was then transferred to a volunteer from the Multnomah County Victims Assistance Program, who talked to the woman until the police and the ambulance arrived at her apartment complex 10 minutes later.

She was still crying and shivering as she told the officers about the attack.

"What did he look like?" one of them asked.

"I didn't get to see him really well. It was dark, and he told me not to look at his face—I was afraid to disobey him because he had a knife at my throat. But he was white, with dark hair. Probably mid- to late-20s, slender and not too tall…maybe five-foot-eight, or five-foot-ten at the most," she replied, giving as much detail as she could. The vague description was handed over to Detective David Foesch from the Portland Police Bureau's sex crimes unit, and although he tried to get more specifics from the victim, that was all she could tell him.

She was then taken to the hospital, examined for injury, and given a tranquilizer. Hair samples were taken from various parts of her body, along with vaginal swabs, and she was escorted back home, still visibly rattled and upset.

A month later, in early February, Stevenson struck again. Sometime between 2:30 and 3:30 AM, he entered the home of a 24-year-old woman, again in the Mount Scott neighborhood, and again through an unlocked door. He crawled into bed with her, waking her up.

She gasped, and Stevenson put a sock in her mouth. "Keep quiet," he told her, showing her his knife to make sure she cooperated. "I won't hurt you if you do what I say." Then he tied her hands and put a pair of pantyhose over her face, wrapping the legs around her eyes so she wouldn't be able to see his face.

While she lay there helpless, Stevenson ripped off her sleepwear, then took his knife and cut off her panties. When she was naked, he ran the point of his knife over her body, leaving small cuts. Then he raped her violently and tried to sodomize her, but ran away when the attempt failed. After waiting a while to be sure he was really gone, and after her heart stopped racing, the victim called the police.

When they heard her description of what had just happened, investigators were pretty sure that it was the same rapist who had struck in January. But he wasn't leaving any clues behind, and without a better description, they had no leads to go on.

By April, Stevenson had made two more rape attempts, entering apartments in Mount Scott through unlocked doors as before. But these women hadn't been as easy to subdue as his first two victims, and they had screamed so loudly and so consistently that he had to give up and leave both times.

But to make matters worse for investigators, Stevenson wasn't the only rapist on the loose. Maybe they were copying Stevenson's crimes, or maybe it was coincidence, but a whole slew of unsolved rapes were popping up on officials' lists in all corners of Portland and East Multnomah County. Investigators compared the attacks, including the methods the rapists had used and their outcomes, to see if the Mount Scott rapist may have been committing those, too. Then they cross-referenced their information with reported rapes in Clackamas and Yamhill counties, the cities of Beaverton and Lake Oswego, and outlying areas of Washington State. But just when they thought their slate was full, another rape occurred, which brings us back to April 20, 1983.

Stevenson had been sitting on his latest victim's bed for some time now, telling her all about the problems in his life.

"What do you do for fun?" she had asked.

"I play pool," he answered. "For money. I win a lot at the tavern I go to."

"Oh, that's cool," she offered, faking interest. "What's it called?"

When Stevenson told her the name of his favorite pool hall, she didn't show recognition, but knew that it was just a few blocks away.

"Well, I gotta go now," Stevenson told her. "Don't call the cops. I'm warning you, I'll know if you do."

"Don't worry, I won't," the woman assured him. As an afterthought, she reached for her dresser and grabbed a business card from a short stack. "Here's my card. You can call me if you want."

Stevenson hesitated, but then stuck the card in his pocket and left her apartment. As soon as she was sure he was gone, she broke her promise and called the police. Her description of him wasn't much better than the others, but it was enough for them to know that they were dealing with the Mount Scott rapist.

"Oh, and…I gave him my business card," she revealed. "I was hoping you could monitor my phone in case he decides to call me."

Like the previous victims, she was taken to the hospital for testing and vaginal swabs. When dipped in acid phosphatase, the swabs turned bright purple, indicating the presence of semen. More samples were then taken to test for the rapist's blood type.

Since he had spent so much time in the woman's apartment, investigators thought they might find more clues there than in the others, but their search turned up very little, and detectives decided that their perpetrator was either very careful or very lucky…or maybe both. But the thing about luck is that it can change at any time—the only question is when.

By the end of June, Stevenson had raped two more victims, but this time they were males. As he had done before, he attacked between 2:30 and 3:30 AM, threatening his victims with a knife and stuffing socks in their mouths so they couldn't yell out. He tied his victims' hands with a phone cord and, in both cases, lubricated himself and raped them anally.

Both victims reported the incidents to the police, and suddenly the case was in the spotlight and making media headlines. Police admitted that since men were less likely to report being sexually assaulted than women, it was possible that the Mount Scott rapist had violated more victims than they knew about.

The director of the Multnomah County Victims Assistance Program announced publically, "The way our society approaches rape and sodomy, we've thought women were the victims. It's very difficult for men to report...but when people see normal men in their homes and some individual decides to attack them, it shows that it can happen to anyone."

The police issued urgent warnings to Mount Scott residents, who were both afraid and angry to learn about what had been happening right under their noses. Residents were informed that a rapist was on the loose in their neighborhood, attacking people who lived alone, right in their own beds. A sheriff's department press release described the suspect as being a white male, 20 to 30 years old, five-foot-eight to six feet in height, with a thin to medium build. He had longish brown hair, covering his ears and shirt collar, and maybe a thin mustache.

In response, neighbors rallied together and started looking out for each other, getting more involved in their neighborhood associations. "It's almost a blessing in disguise," said an area coordinator for Neighborhoods Against Crime. "They need to get organized, and this is doing it. I'm sorry that something this serious is what it takes."

Flyers were printed up and circulated throughout the community. Some advertised self-defense classes for women and girls who were at least 10 years old, and others were issued by the police, describing the suspect and urging people to call 911 if they had anything to report. The Mount Scott Neighborhood Association helped the cause by distributing the flyers door to door and noticed that people were extra cautious about opening their doors to receive them.

However, at least one resident wasn't at all sympathetic to the victims. "It's their fault if they're that stupid not to lock their doors nowadays," he said.

Meanwhile, investigators started finding patterns among all the various incidents that allowed them to pinpoint at least six other rapes and two attempted rapes that had been committed by the Mount Scott rapist, and to eliminate numerous other ones that were not his doing. This was thanks to cooperation between the Portland Police Bureau and the sheriff's departments from Multnomah, Clackamas and Yamhill counties. As it turned out, the Mount Scott rapist really did seem to be striking only in the Mount Scott area, but they still didn't have enough information to identify a possible suspect.

By the middle of July, the Guardian Angels started patrolling Mount Scott in the early mornings. The Guardian Angels are a not-for-profit volunteer safety patrol organization, originally founded in New York, whose members walk the streets of many major cities, and before the attacks, they had primarily focused on the downtown transit mall area. But after finding out about the string of rapes, they stationed some of their troops in the Mount Scott area. The founder of their Portland chapter said, "We read the articles in the paper and wanted residents to know that we're not just concerned about the downtown area, so we volunteered our services. We don't want people to have to change the way they live because some crazy guy is on the loose."

While the Angels kept an eye on the southeast Portland neighborhood, more rapes were occurring in the southwest. An overly trusting 13-year-old girl was asked to help clean the home of a male family friend, and he raped her. Before police had a chance to arrest him, he had attacked two more women, aged 19 and 23. He raped the first and sodomized the second, then forced them at knifepoint to perform sexual acts on each other, threatening their lives if they didn't comply.

Finally, 27-year-old David Isaac Maimon was arrested and charged with first-degree rape, sodomy and sexual abuse. While in custody, police investigated whether he could also be the Mount Scott rapist; he was the right age, after all, and he did use a knife. But the Mount Scott attacks continued while Maimon was in jail, so he was taken off the suspect list. He later pleaded innocent to the rape charges laid against him, but he ended up being convicted and was sentenced to prison.

Another lead revolved around a 24-year-old woman who was abducted at knifepoint from downtown Portland at 3:30 AM on Saturday, December 3, forced into a car, and gagged and tied up with surgical tape. Then she was raped under the Ross Island Bridge, cut several times with the knife and had her life threatened, before being released in Clackamas County's Cottonwood Park. A 21-year-old Portland man was arrested for the incident a week later and charged with several crimes, but he was eventually eliminated as a Mount Scott rapist suspect.

Then a 20-year-old woman was raped in Beaverton by a man who climbed through an unlocked window into her apartment on Southwest Jamieson Road at about 1:00 AM. He threatened her with a knife, forced her to strip naked, tied her hands behind her back and fondled her, before violently raping her. When he hurried off after the attack, she called the police, but despite the similarities, investigators were sure that the crime hadn't been committed by the Mount Scott rapist.

There was another incident, however, that had his mark on it. At around 11:30 PM one night, Stevenson had burst into a woman's apartment on Southeast 20th Place, grabbed a knife from the kitchen and took hold of the woman and her baby son. He wrapped his right arm around her neck, and she noticed the tattoo on it, but she didn't recall ever seeing him before. Apparently Stevenson knew her, though, because he kept calling her by her name. He made her sodomize herself, threatening to slice both her and her son with the knife if she didn't obey, then raped her and penetrated her with a foreign object.

After he took off, she called the police in a panic. She said the attack had gone on for about 20 minutes and that she had gotten a good enough look at him to identify him if she ever saw him again. She described him as having brown hair, a mustache and acne scars. It wasn't enough to arrest anyone, but her description was the most detailed one to date.

On January 29, 1984—a little more than a year after the first rape—another one occurred, but this time in Lake

Oswego, near the intersection of Southwest Longfellow Road and Childs Road. The perpetrator entered a woman's home early in the morning, sexually assaulted her and then stole some of her jewelry. She said her attacker was white, 25 to 30 years old, about five-foot-seven and 165 pounds, with blond hair, a mustache and a pockmarked complexion. The Clackamas County Sheriff's Department shared this description with the Portland Police Bureau because the pockmarked skin could have been from acne scars, but the rest of the description didn't quite match the others, so they weren't able to definitely say that it had been the Mount Scott rapist.

Then things slowed down, and while authorities continued to try to connect the dots from various cases and create a profile of the rapist, they weren't getting very far. What they didn't know was that the Mount Scott rapist had just split from his wife and had left the area.

In March 1984, Stevenson went on his first date with a woman who was to become his new girlfriend, Cindy Becker. Eventually, they moved into an apartment together in downtown Portland.

Becker wasn't sure about Stevenson. When things were good, she adored him, but sometimes, even as far back as that first date, she had visions of him being the type of guy who could be violent towards women. One night, she asked him about it, and Stevenson broke down into sobs.

"Cindy, you don't know...you just don't know," he choked out haltingly, cradling his head in his hands. "What you've been seeing is that I'm...I'm the Mount Scott rapist."

Becker recoiled slightly, looking Stevenson in the eye to
see if he was telling the truth. "What do you mean?" she
asked, frightened.

"I used to stay downtown after I got off work," he
confessed, his voice cracking. "Last year, after I'd been
drinking a few times, I stopped off in a few apartments on
my way home. I was going to do some burglaries...you
know, just steal a few things. But then I found the people in
bed, and I...I raped them. I tied them up and raped them."

Becker was torn between feeling sorry for Stevenson and
being disgusted and horrified over what he had done, but
above all she was frightened for her own safety. Soon the
two of them broke up, and Becker decided to turn him in,
both so that he couldn't harm any more people and so that
he could get the help he needed.

"I believe my ex-boyfriend is the Mount Scott rapist,"
she told the police. "He confessed to me that he committed
the crimes." It was the lead investigators had been waiting
for the past two years.

Detective Foesch went to Stevenson's apartment in the
900 block of Southwest Salmon Street in downtown
Portland and arrested him for the Mount Scott rapes, locking
him up in the Justice Center jail with a bail amount of
$250,000.

On Monday, March 18, and Tuesday, March 19, Stevenson
was put in criminal lineups along with five other men who
had similar characteristics, all dressed in the same type of
clothes. Two of the victims of the Mount Scott rapist fingered
Stevenson as being the perpetrator.

After the lineups, Stevenson was charged with 14 felony
crimes, including six counts of rape, four of burglary, two of

attempted sodomy and one each of sodomy and unlawful sexual penetration. He pleaded innocent, but was told that there might be future charges coming from other lineups.

On Monday June 10, 1985, Stevenson's first trial started in the Multnomah County Circuit Court, with Judge Donald Kalberer presiding. Deputy District Attorney John Foote gave the jurors the background of the case, focusing on the southeast Portland rape that occurred on April 20, 1983.

The woman who had been raped—the one that had encouraged Stevenson to talk about his personal life after the attack—pointed right at him with utmost confidence. "That's him…there's no doubt in my mind," she told the courtroom. Then she gave the details of her two-and-a-half-hour ordeal for the jury.

Stevenson's attorney, Angel Lopez, claimed that the state didn't have any conclusive physical evidence to link Stevenson to the crime, and that the victim had wrongly identified his client. He argued that if it had been Stevenson, she would have surely noticed his broken nose, deep acne scars and the tattoo on his shoulder. Apparently, Lopez ignored the fact that the whole event had taken place in the dark, where those details would not have been so obvious, and that the victim had been repeatedly warned not to look at his face, which meant she could only steal glances here and there.

It also turned out that most of the victims had underestimated his size; Stevenson was actually six-foot-two and closer to 200 pounds. But if those facts added any doubt to the proceedings, they were quickly expunged when a prosecuting witness confirmed that Stevenson had lived in Mount Scott when the attacks took place, and that when

Stevenson had seen the police composite drawing, he had commented that he thought he knew who the Mount Scott rapist might be. He also added that Stevenson's marital problems at the time had been common knowledge and that he did indeed play pool for money at the local tavern that the victim had named. As a final nail in his coffin, Cindy Becker then testified that Stevenson had confessed the crimes to her.

Prosecutor Foote reminded the jury in his closing arguments that the information revealed to the victim by her attacker on April 20, 1983, matched Robert Stevenson's identity "on at least 33 points." He admitted that the state wasn't able to produce any physical evidence but that the victim herself served as proof beyond any reasonable doubts. "Every woman this man has touched, he has hurt," he continued. "It's time to end that pain and find him guilty."

The jurors deliberated for three and a half hours, then delivered their verdict: guilty on four counts of first-degree rape and one count each of burglary and attempted first-degree sodomy. And that was just the beginning—there were three additional trials with multiple sex-related charges waiting in the wings. Stevenson was later convicted of two other counts of first-degree rape, another count of burglary, as well as unlawful sexual penetration, sodomy and attempted sodomy.

Judge Kalberer had a pre-sentencing investigation report created before he sentenced Stevenson to six years in prison for the sodomy attempt, 18 years each for one burglary and one rape, and the maximum sentences for the other crimes, including 20 years each for the six rapes. Stevenson began his prison sentences for all counts on October 17, 1985.

He was later moved to the Snake River Correctional Institution in Ontario, Oregon, after it opened in 1991, and at the time of writing has no foreseeable parole date.

CHAPTER TEN

Gary Leon Ridgway
The Green River Killer
(1949–)

All crime is a kind of disease and should be treated as such.

—Mahatma Gandhi (1869–1948), Indian political and spiritual leader

"Let's do a half and half," he said to the girl on his bed. "I'll, uh, pay you extra for it...first the, uh, oral sex, and then intercourse."

"Okay," she agreed. "An extra $20."

"And, uh, I'd like to see you naked." He knew that she'd feel more vulnerable that way. But this wasn't the average-guy Gary Ridgway that everyone knew, the one who had been a loyal employee to a single company for many years; this was the secret Gary Ridgway—the one better known as the Green River Killer. In fact, for two decades, this secret Gary Ridgway was *only* known as the Green River Killer, since nobody could figure out who the man behind the moniker was.

Now the man was behind the girl—in this case it was 18-year-old Marie Malvar—and things went pretty much the same way as it did with most of his victims. "I can only, uh, have an orgasm if I—if I'm behind you," he had explained, kneeling on the bed as he entered her. Now he watched for her to raise her head as he finished.

As soon as she did, he grabbed her in a chokehold, then wrapped her pantyhose around her neck and twisted them tight. The girl gasped and started to panic as she realized that what had started out as a routine trick had just turned dangerous...even deadly.

"Please, don't kill me!" she begged, struggling against Ridgway's grasp. She thought about her younger sister, Marilyn, who was sick at home and expecting her back. Ridgway tightened his grip, and she reached up to scratch his arm.

"You're hurting me! I'm too young to die!" Malvar cried out.

"I'm sorry, I—I didn't mean to hurt you. If you stop struggling, I'll let you go," Ridgway promised. As soon as she went limp, he quickly strangled her to death. Then he clipped her fingernails so his skin cells wouldn't be found under them and removed her earrings and bracelet—he would leave those in the women's restroom at his work later, to see which of his co-workers ended up wearing them. Then he nonchalantly got ready to dispose of her body.

It was April 30, 1983, and the Green River Killer had killed again, for the twenty-first time, but to him it was just another day on the job in what he considered a long "career." Ridgway certainly knew a few things about dedication and longevity, but hardly anybody would have thought he knew anything about killing.

Gary Leon Ridgway was born in Salt Lake City, Utah, on February 18, 1949, to Thomas and Mary Ridgway. He was the second of three sons; Greg was a year older, and Thomas was two years younger. When Gary was 11 years old, the Ridgway clan moved to Washington State and settled in the McMicken Heights neighborhood, which was across the highway from the Seattle-Tacoma International Airport and next to the Green River. That section of the Pacific Highway South was known as the Sea-Tac Strip—or just "The Strip"—and was the main route between Seattle and Tacoma.

In school, Ridgway was remembered as having a bright smile, if not a bright mind; he was friendly and polite, but his grades were poor and his IQ was low. As a teenager, he tagged along with his brother Greg, smoking cigarettes and trying to act tough, but he always ended up just blending in with his surroundings.

During adolescence, Ridgway displayed what researchers call the "deadly triangle" often found in serial killers: long-term bed-wetting, arson and animal cruelty. Ridgway wet the bed until age 13, set fires a few times as a teenager and once suffocated a cat to death. At 16, he asked six-year-old Jimmy Davis if he wanted to play, then led him into the woods and stabbed him in the ribs.

"Why'd you kill me?" asked a confused Jimmy, seeing the blood running down his side and leg.

Ridgway laughed and wiped the blade of the knife off on Jimmy's shoulder. "I always wanted to know what it felt like to kill somebody," he replied, before walking off.

Jimmy survived but needed a major operation to repair the damage to his liver and spent several weeks in the hospital. He never went back to school, charges were never laid and Jimmy's family moved to California a few months later.

Just before graduating from high school, Ridgway got a job painting trucks at the Kenworth Truck Co. in Renton and worked there for over 30 years, except for the two years that he spent in the Navy. He was always a hard-working employee and was even given perfect attendance awards. He seemed like your average, harmless type of guy: five-foot-ten, 150 pounds, brown hair and glasses, usually wearing jeans and a T-shirt. He got along well with all his co-workers and never strayed too far from his parents. Throughout his adult life, he lived in several places along the South Pacific Highway, near his childhood home.

His love life, however, was a little stormier. Ridgway was married three times, with the first wedding taking place a year after he graduated from high school, on August 15, 1970. His bride, Claudia Kraig, was 20 years old, and he was 21. Soon after, they moved to San Diego for his stint in the Navy, and he went out to sea for six months. During that time, Kraig had an affair with one of their mutual friends, and Ridgway later said she had become a "whore." He was discharged in 1971 and returned to Washington, only to learn of the affair; even though they tried to work it out, the couple divorced in early 1972.

Later that year, Ridgway met Marcia Winslow, and they were married on December 14, 1973. They often rode their bikes along the Green River, stopping occasionally to have sex in the grass; in fact, she later said that he only saw her as a sex object. They had one son together, Matthew, who was born on September 5, 1975.

After Matthew's birth, Ridgway became extremely religious and made the family attend several churches; he was known to cry during services and went door to door to spread the word of God. On the other hand, Winslow said, he would do strange and alarming things at home, like sneaking up behind her and putting her in a chokehold. After the couple separated in 1980, Ridgway's religious fanaticism came to an end.

In July 1980, he was picked up by police after a prostitute said he had choked her, but he was let go after claiming that she provoked the incident by biting him while performing oral sex. The next day, the police were called in to break up a physical fight between Ridgway and Winslow. When they filed for divorce in 1981, they each took out a restraining order; in fact, Ridgway later said that if he had only been able to kill her, it would have stopped him from murdering other women.

And sure enough, soon afterwards, Ridgway embarked upon his infamous killing spree. Nobody really knows how many women Ridgway killed—not even him. "I killed so many women, I have a hard time keeping them straight," he told the court during his trial. He pleaded guilty to strangling 48 young women and teenage girls, but the list could have contained 55 victims, and many officials think he murdered up to twice that number. In any case, Ridgway is considered to be America's most prolific serial killer, and his rampage was the longest on record. For 20 years, the identity of the Green River Killer was a total mystery, until Ridgway finally confessed in 2003.

But could it really have all been because of misdirected anger towards his ex-wife? Although this certainly seems to be a major factor, it can't be the only one. Ridgway had always had an ongoing love-hate relationship with prostitutes, who became his usual victims—he didn't like them hanging around his neighborhood but would proposition their services and had been doing so since he had been in the Navy. At one point, he admitted to being fixated with—even addicted to—prostitutes, and yet said in the same breath that he despised them.

His dislike of prostitutes may have had something to do with his first wife, whom he repeatedly called a whore, or his second wife, the "sex object" he wanted to kill, but it could also have been because of a similar love-hate relationship with his mother. He visited her often, which was easy to do because he lived so close, but his mother dominated him in the same way she dominated his father, and neither of them was ever able to please her. Ridgway always asked her before he would buy anything, even after he got married, and kept her name on his checking account for years.

"I've always had a sexual attraction towards my mother," Ridgway would later tell detectives. "She made me feel lust, and she made me feel humiliation. Sometimes I wanted to stab her."

Ridgway's mother dressed in tight clothing and was sometimes described as looking very much like a prostitute. She abused his father constantly, doing things like smashing a dinner plate over his head and then just silently walking away. Chances are his father felt humiliated by his wife, too. But although Ridgway later identified with his father's feelings, he never took his dad's side; he was always a mama's boy.

Maybe Ridgway's guilt over his attraction to his mother, or his anger over her constant humiliation of him, drove him too far. Or perhaps it was a case of the Oedipus complex gone wild, where instead of figuratively sleeping with his mother and killing his father, Ridgway chose to both sleep with and kill his mother—again and again and again.

Some of his victims were runaways, but most of them were prostitutes; in either case, he would choose women that nobody would look for if they went missing. To him, they were disposable—a dime a dozen, though he didn't even want to pay that much for them—and FBI profiler John Douglas was spot on when he concluded that the Green River Killer left his victims' bodies near dumping areas, or partially covered with garbage or leaves, because he thought of them as being "human garbage."

This is typical of a psychopath—a lack of empathy to the point where he has absolutely no respect for his victims, and it wasn't worth knowing their names or trying to differentiate them from one another. Ridgway couldn't even remember *when* he killed them—he said he may have even killed one or two in the '70s—but he did remember killing them, usually in his house or his truck, and he knew exactly where every body could be found.

After divorcing Winslow, Ridgway had a number of girl-friends and each of them—like Winslow—said he had an insatiable sexual appetite, wanting to make love several times a day. He lived with Nancy Palmer for about six months in 1981, and then started seeing Sharon Hebert around December. On Christmas Eve, he confessed to her that he had just almost killed a prostitute, but surprisingly, she didn't leave him until six months later. It wasn't until yet another of Ridgway's girlfriends, Roxanne Theno, told Hebert that Ridgway had given her herpes after sleeping with numerous prostitutes that Hebert dumped him. Interestingly, Theno stayed with Ridgway and almost married him in June 1984. He met all three women at various Parents Without Partners events.

Shortly after Ridgway and Hebert broke up, on July 7, 1982, 36-year-old Amina Agisheff disappeared while walking home from a downtown Seattle restaurant where she worked as a waitress. Her remains weren't found until two years later, and while Ridgway has never been charged with her murder, she's always been considered one of the Green River Killer's first victims—even though her circumstances were different than those of most of the others.

Agisheff was older than Ridgway's other victims, in a healthy relationship, and was neither a prostitute nor a runaway. Agisheff was the type of woman who would be missed and had loved ones looking for her right after her disappearance—and that may have been why she was the only such victim. Later, when talking about his typical prey, Ridgway said he picked prostitutes because, "I knew they would not be reported missing right away and might never be reported missing. I picked prostitutes because I thought I could kill as many of them as I wanted without getting caught."

Economic times were tough, and The Strip was full of young women trading sex for cash. He would spend hours driving up and down the street—"patrolling" as he called it—for the right women, the one that he thought would be the easiest to kill. Typically, they were young and fairly naïve, rather than street-smart career prostitutes. While he preferred white women, he wasn't too choosy because he figured he'd soon be discarding them, anyhow.

Ridgway would gain their trust by showing them pictures of his young son and leaving toys on his dashboard. Sometimes he would befriend them further by becoming a regular customer for a while, giving them rides or promising to get them jobs. When he picked them up, he would do so in a nearby parking lot after driving by and flashing money, rather than along the curb where he might be spotted by witnesses.

Some of his victims often said he looked like an undercover cop, so he started carrying beer in his truck to ease their fears—but apparently they didn't think he looked like a killer. At least 50 of them also asked him straight out if he was the Green River Killer, to which he responded, "Uh, do I look like the Green River Killer?" If they only had thought "Yes!" they might still be alive.

Ridgway would offer extra money to go somewhere private, and he would sometimes have a spare tire in the front seat as proof that they needed more space. The ones that agreed were the ones that he killed, but those that were hesitant would be let go after performing their services. Not only did that instill trust for next time, but he saw it as valuable insurance and future proof that he was just a regular, kind-hearted john—a "good date"—who would never hurt the girls. After killing one, he'd ask for her again next time to make it seem as if he didn't know a thing.

The day after Agisheff went missing, Ridgway strangled 16-year-old Wendy Lee Coffield, who had last been seen leaving her foster home in Tacoma to go visit her grandfather. A week later, her body was found in the Green

River, just north of the Meeker Street Bridge in Kent. Two days after Coffield disappeared, Ridgway strangled 17-year-old prostitute Gisele Ann Lovvorn with a pair of socks. Her body was found two months later, south of the airport, with her blonde hair dyed black.

On July 25, 1982, 23-year-old Debra Bonner left a motel on The Strip and was killed by Ridgway; her body was dumped in the Green River in Kent only to be found slumped over a log almost three weeks later. On August 1, he killed 31-year-old Marcia Chapman, a mother of two, and threw her body in the Green River, too. It was found two weeks later, on August 15, along with the body of 17-year-old Cynthia Hinds, who had disappeared on August 11—both bodies had been weighted down with rocks. The body of Cynthia's friend, 16-year-old Opal Mills, was found the same day in a nearby grassy area, with bruises on her arms and legs and her pants tied around her neck. She had last been seen just a few days earlier. Bob Pedrin, a former classmate of Ridgway's who had played football with him and was now a Fire District 43 firefighter and a member of the underwater rescue team, was called to the scene but had no idea how close a tie he had to the perpetrator of these gruesome crimes.

This was Ridgway's first "cluster" of bodies. He liked to dispose of several bodies in the same area because it made it easier to find out if they had been discovered, which made him avoid using that spot again in the future. He also demonstrated typical serial killer behavior, such as driving by or returning to the scene of the crime to reenact in his mind what he'd done—something that gave him a feeling of power he didn't have in his everyday life—or even having sex with the dead bodies, which he later admitted to. What he didn't do was keep "trophies," such as body parts or jewelry, as some serial killers do; if he had, he would certainly have been caught much sooner. However, Ridgway considered the bodies "his"—whether they were "trash" or not, they were "his" trash, under his control—and he hated when they were taken away from him.

After the first cluster was discovered, Ridgway started hiding his bodies better, and most of them weren't found until months or years after the victims disappeared. But meanwhile, police realized that they were dealing with a serial killer and put together a special task force of King County detectives—the largest since the Ted Bundy murders eight years earlier. It was headed by Major Richard Kraske and Detective Dave Reichert, with help from FBI serial killer profiler John Douglas and criminal investigator Bob Keppel, who had worked on the Bundy case and would eventually enlist Bundy's help from death row with this investigation.

Unfortunately, since they didn't trust the police, many of the prostitutes who could have offered vital information or possible leads were reluctant to talk.

On August 29, Ridgway killed 16-year-old Terry Milligan. The day before, 16-year-old Kase Ann Lee also went missing, but while she was likely killed by Ridgway, her body has never been found. On September 15, 19-year-old Mary Meehan—who was almost eight months pregnant—was abducted and murdered while she was out for a walk. That let another Green River Killer suspect, a butcher named Charles Clinton Clark, off the hook because he was in custody at the time after having raped two young women at gunpoint.

The next suspect that investigators targeted was Melvyn Foster, a 44-year-old taxi driver who had worked The Strip and happened to fit Douglas's profile: a confident, middle-aged, religious man who was familiar with the area, who would frequent the murder scenes to relive the events and who even offered to assist the police. To further the suspicions against him, he failed a lie detector test, but he was also under surveillance while another series of murders took place.

On September 20, 15-year-old Debra Estes was killed, followed by 16-year-old Linda Rule on September 26—the same day that Lovvorn's body was found with black-dyed hair. In the last three months of 1982, Ridgway killed four more women: 23-year-old Denise Bush, 17-year-old Shawnda Summers, 18-year-old Shirley Sherrill and 15-year-old Colleen Brockman, who disappeared on Christmas Eve. After killing them, Ridgway drove the bodies of Bush and Sherrill to Tigard, Oregon, where they were found in the summer of 1984.

On November 9, one of Ridgway's intended victims, Rebecca Garde Guay, managed to escape after being violently choked in his truck. Unfortunately, she didn't report the incident for another two years, or the killings might have stopped. When she finally spoke up, Ridgway repeated the excuse he had used before—that she had bitten him during oral sex—which she denied.

Ridgway did stop killing for a month or two and was stopped by police on February 23, 1983, for having 18-year-old prostitute Keli McGinness in his truck—a girl who later disappeared. He started murdering again with a vengeance in the spring, apparently wanting to make up for lost time. He killed 18-year-old Alma Smith on March 3, 1983, and then went back to the same spot an hour later to hunt again. He tried to pick up her friend, Cynthia Bassett-Ornelas, but she refused because she had seen him leaving with Smith. He gave up and went home, then waited a week or two before killing his next victim, 17-year-old Delores Williams.

In the month of April, he murdered 23-year-old Gail Mathews, 19-year-old Andrea Childers, 17-year-old Sandra Gabbert, 16-year-old Kimi-Kai Pitsor and 18-year-old Marie Malvar. The last one was the murder that should have put him behind bars.

On April 30, 1983, Malvar's boyfriend and pimp, Robert Woods, watched her argue with the driver of a dark-colored truck, but she still got inside. Worried about her, he followed the truck as it sped off, but eventually lost it at a stoplight. He never saw Malvar again but kept looking for her with the help of her father, Jose Malvar. A few days later, Jose saw the same dark truck parked at Ridgway's home on South 348th Street and gave the address to police. When the cops came calling, Ridgway said he'd never seen Marie before and, incredibly, they seemed satisfied with his answer and left. They failed to notice the scratches on his arm, which he later disguised by burning his forearm with battery acid. Rumor went that the pretty girl must have just moved to Hollywood or Hawaii, and the truth wouldn't be known for another 20 years.

Gail Mathews' boyfriend had also seen his girlfriend get into a similar truck—a dark green one that Ridgway had borrowed from his brother and would later repaint—and reported her disappearance when she failed to return, but somehow the police never connected the two incidents.

By this time, the task force was becoming frustrated, and Bob Keppel wrote up a report for King County Sheriff Vern Thomas that was critical of how the case was being handled. Tips and evidence were strewn all over the place with no way to cross-reference them, and the cost of the investigation—already the largest in history—was about to climb even higher just to reorganize it all.

Part of the reason it was hard to catch Ridgway was that he never left any clues behind that could be used to identify him, but he did plant some red herrings. Besides clipping a girl's fingernails if she scratched him and being careful not to leave fingerprints, he'd often leave somebody else's cigarettes or chewed gum at the scene of the crime. To cover his tracks with Malvar, he went back and threw around some leaflets from airport motels so that a traveling businessman would be suspected. Another time, he left some plastic tubing and broken pencils, and a third time he dropped a hair pick like the ones pimps often used.

With 21-year-old Carol Ann Christensen, the red herring was actually a trout. The young mother was another victim who worked at a tavern on The Strip rather than as a prostitute, and she was last seen leaving work. Ridgway abducted her on May 3, 1983, and her body was found five days later. Morbidly, he had posed her body with some items taken from her house: two trout on her chest, a paper bag over her head, ground meat on her hand and a wine bottle on her stomach.

The killings continued throughout the summer with the deaths of 18-year-old Martina Authorlee, 18-year-old Cheryl

Lee Wims, 19-year-old Yvonne Antosh, 15-year-old Carrie Rois, 20-year-old Constance Naon, 22-year-old Kelly Ware, 22-year-old Tina Thompson and 17-year-old April Buttram. A 16-year-old girl named Tammie Liles and 18-year-old Keli McGinness—the prostitute seen in his truck back in February—also went missing, and they're both presumed to be victims of Ridgway, even though their bodies have never been found. A body that was found that summer, however, belonged to Shawnda Summers.

From September to December 1983, seven more bodies were found, and nine more women went missing. Patricia Osborn, who was 19 years old, is another presumed victim who's never been found, while the rest were definitely killed by Ridgway: 26-year-old Debbie Abernathy, 19-year-old Tracy Ann Wilson, 19-year-old Maureen Feeney, 25-year-old Mary Bello, 16-year-old Pammy Avent, 22-year-old Delise Plager, 20-year-old Kimberly Nelson and 19-year-old Lisa Yates.

The cluster of bodies that police found next were those of Delores Williams, Gail Matthews, Yvonne Antosh, Constance Naon, Kelly Ware, Kimi-Kai Pitsor—at least, her skull—and Mary Meehan, who, along with her unborn baby, was the only victim that Ridgway left fully buried.

In response to the growing murders, the Green River Task Force increased in size, and Captain Frank Adamson took over the lead in January 1984.

From then on, they focused on a possible suspect's innocence rather than his guilt so they could immediately eliminate those that had alibis and whittle down their leads. They also began to piece together certain patterns, noticing that almost all the victims disappeared from The Strip or downtown Seattle and that most of them had a history of prostitution. Dumping grounds for the clusters of bodies had moved from the Green River to the Sea-Tac Airport and Star Lake in 1983, then to the Mountain View Cemetery in Auburn and North Bend near Interstate 90 in 1984—presumably areas near the killer's home. And perhaps most importantly, they finally found a definite clue: a man's size 10 or 11 shoe print near one of the bodies.

On February 6, Ridgway killed 16-year-old Mary West, who was last seen in South Seattle. On March 13, he picked up 17-year-old hitchhiker Cindy Anne Smith on The Strip, but instead of giving her a ride, he brutally murdered her—and for the next 19 years, it was thought that she was the last victim of the Green River Killer.

On February 14, police found the body of Denise Plager, followed over the next several months by Cheryl Wims, Lisa Yates, Debbie Abernathy, Terry Milligan, Sandra Gabbert, Alma Smith, Amina Agisheff, Colleen Brockman and another victim who has never been identified. Interestingly, Task Force volunteer and psychic Barbara Kubik-Patten found Tina Thompson's body in April, based on a vision she had, but police didn't tap into her services after that. However, they did take up Ted Bundy on his offer to help give insight into a serial killer's mind and build the Green River Killer's profile.

Meanwhile, a prostitute named Dawn White suggested that Ridgway could be a suspect based on his "weird" nature, so he was investigated again. On May 7, however, he successfully passed a polygraph test and was cleared as a suspect—though it was later determined that the test was incomplete, so the results weren't valid. White and her pimp also had a private meeting with Ridgway; she thought he acted guilty during the whole conversation, and after that he did stop killing for a while. Then he almost married girlfriend Roxanne Theno in June, but she soon left him for another man—something that he didn't really seem concerned about.

In the fall of 1984, the remains of Mary Bello and Martina Authorlee were found near Highway 410. In November, Rebecca Garde Guay finally came forward to tell the Task Force that Ridgway had choked her in 1982—and he admitted to it after they reopened his file and tracked him down again in February 1985. He also acknowledged that he "dated" prostitutes, including possibly some of the victims, but still he eluded capture. That year he met and started dating—in the conventional sense—Judith Lynch, the woman who would become his third and final wife three years later.

In March 1985, the body of Carrie Rois was discovered near Star Lake Road, and then in June, a bulldozer operator found the bodies that had been planted in Oregon. The Oregon cluster allowed the FBI to get involved in a greater capacity since it was now an interstate case. Falling victim to another of Ridgway's red herrings, the Task Force then focused their efforts on Portland for a few months. It would be six months before any more bodies were found: Mary West, the rest of Kimi-Kai Pitsor's remains and another unidentified young woman.

Throughout 1986, public consensus was that the Task Force was a monumental joke, even with FBI backup. Understandably, people were both scared and angry about the lack of results. Another suspect, a trapper named Bill McLean, was questioned and then released, while Ridgway told the police he hadn't been with prostitutes in over 18 months because he kept catching venereal diseases from them. He agreed to another lie detector test but never had to take it because his lawyer told the FBI to leave him alone. For some reason, they listened and again stopped investigating him.

The remains of several more victims were found that year, including Tracy Winston, Maureen Feeney and Kimberly Nelson. Paige Miley, a prostitute who had known Nelson, told the Task Force that Ridgway had been Nelson's last date, which reopened his file yet again. This time they went to his ex-wife, Marcia Winslow, who showed them some of his favorite places to have sex—which happened to be some of the same areas as the Green River Killer's dumping grounds.

On October 17, Ridgway struck again, killing 19-year-old Patricia Barczak; her body wasn't found for over six years.

By the end of the year, the number of Task Force staff had been reduced by almost half, and Captain James Pompey had taken over leadership. Right after that, in December, two more bodies were found in the woods, but much farther away than all the others—in fact, they were in a different country altogether, northeast of Vancouver, British Columbia, in Canada.

On February 7, 1987, Ridgway picked up 21-year-old Roberta Hayes after her release from an Oregon jail on prostitution charges and promptly killed her. Her remains weren't found for another five years. In April, investigators got a search warrant for Ridgway's house, vehicles and lockers at work, and he gave them his hair and saliva for DNA samples—but even with all that evidence, the

Washington State Patrol Crime Lab was still unable to firmly link him to any of the Green River crimes. However, they did scare him and his murders slowed down again.

On May 30, 1988, construction workers found the remains of Debra Estes in Federal Way, where Ridgway had discarded them over five years earlier. Almost two weeks later, on June 12, 38-year-old Ridgway was married to his third wife, 43-year-old Judith Lynch, on a neighbor's front lawn. In December, a TV special called *Manhunt...Live: A Chance to End the Nightmare* aired, offering $100,000 for any information leading to the Green River Killer's arrest. Over 1500 leads were called in, and the prime suspect, William J. Stevens, a law student in Spokane with a history of burglary, was temporarily jailed a month later on an unrelated charge, then investigated by the Task Force for several months. However, no arrests for the Green River killings were ever made because of the TV show.

In September 1989, Ridgway and Lynch moved to Des Moines, where they'd live until 1997; a month after the move, the body of Andrea Childers was found near the Sea-Tac Airport.

Throughout the 1990s, it seemed that the Green River Killer had stopped hunting for prey and was either in jail or dead himself, so the Task Force was reduced to one detective. However, that wasn't quite the case; in early March 1990, Ridgway killed 36-year-old prostitute and mother of four, Marta Reeves, and her remains were found on September 20. In 1998, he killed 38-year-old Patricia Yellowrobe, but, unusually, he let her get dressed first; when her body was found in a parking lot in August, her death was ruled a drug overdose. During these years, as the

Task Force felt at a loss to find answers, the jailed Happy Face Killer, Keith Hunter Jesperson, was also investigated as a possible suspect.

Ridgway said he was "semi-retired" during this time. In between the two murders, is it really possible that he settled into domestic bliss with his new wife Judith? Could he really have turned into the kind gentleman that she described him as? It could be possible since they gardened, held garage sales, walked their dogs, took RV trips down the coast and read the Bible together. But it's also possible that he was killing other women who we don't know about yet, because he continued to pick up prostitutes and enjoyed the reduced prices of those who were newly addicted to crack. Of course, more bodies started showing up, too: Roberta Hayes in 1991, Nicole French in 1992 and Patricia Barczak in 1993.

Finally, in September 2001, a month after Ridgway's mother died, DNA test results conducted by the Patrol Crime Lab linked Ridgway to three of the Green River Killer victims: Opal Mills, Marcia Chapman and Carol Christensen. For the next few months, detectives quietly watched Ridgway. He was arrested by an undercover cop on November 16 for loitering for the purpose of prostitution and fined $700 on November 27. Then, on November 30, he was arrested as he left work at the Kenworth Truck Company, but this time for good—as a suspect in four Green River killings. After searching his home, vehicles and locker again for a week, police charged Ridgway on December 5 with four counts of aggravated first-degree murder, with Cynthia Hinds being the fourth victim.

On December 18, he pleaded "not guilty" to the charges. His poker face and calm eyes, as always, gave nothing away.

In 2002, while detectives continued building their case against Ridgway, King County Superior Court Judge Richard Jones—brother of music producer Quincy Jones— was chosen to preside over the case, and prosecutor Norm Maleng announced that he would be seeking the death penalty. Ridgway wrote his wife numerous letters of apology from his King County Jail cell in downtown Seattle, and in September, he filed for divorce from her, but she still believed in his innocence.

In March 2003, based on forensic paint evidence from his job, he was charged with three more murders: Wendy Coffield, Debra Estes and Debra Bonner. On April 11, Ridgway finally admitted to his attorneys that he was, in fact, the Green River Killer, and entered into plea negotiations. The plea bargain he ended up with was life imprisonment with no chance of parole instead of the death penalty, in exchange for confessing to all his murders and cooperating with investigators. Families of the victims were outraged— after all, if anyone deserved the death penalty, it should be someone who killed as many people as Ridgway did—but King County officials felt it was more important to bring closure to the previously unsolved cases than to simply kill Ridgway.

On August 16, he led detectives to Pammy Avent's body. Two weeks later, he showed them April Buttram's remains, and a month after that, Marie Malvar. All three of the women had been murdered by Ridgway 20 years earlier, yet he knew exactly where he had left their bodies.

On November 5, 2003, Gary Leon Ridgway pleaded guilty 48 times to murdering all the women, which took almost nine minutes and had Ridgway choking back tears by the end. There could have been seven more names on the list, but Ridgway wasn't completely sure if they were his doing or not. More than half of his victims were teenagers, still trying to figure life out when it was ruthlessly taken from them.

Ridgway is currently serving a sentence of life imprisonment at Washington State Penitentiary in Walla Walla. His case was the most expensive in state history, racking up $13 million for the trial alone and another $15 million for the 20-year investigation. After their experience with the Green River Killer case, investigators in the King County Sheriff's Office are now considered national outdoor crime experts, and other police departments across the country often call on them for help.

CHAPTER ELEVEN

William Dainard
The Child Kidnapper
(1902–92)

Poverty may be the mother of crime, but lack of good sense is the father.

—Jean de la Bruyère (1645–96), French satiric moralist

"Hey, kid, let me ask you something," he called to the nine-year-old boy who had just emerged onto the sidewalk after cutting through the overgrown path bordering the Tacoma Lawn Tennis Club grounds. This chance encounter wasn't expected; it wasn't something they could have planned, even if they had wanted to, but it was better than they could have ever dreamed. They had been watching the family for almost a week, but this was like taking candy from a baby. William Dainard, 33 years old, saw it as a sign regarding the way things should go down: grab George Hunt Weyerhaeuser, heir to the Weyerhaeuser Timber Company fortune, right now on the spot. Then they'd ask his father, John Philip Weyerhaeuser Jr., for a huge ransom payment to get him back.

On Friday, May 24, 1935, George had taken this shortcut on his walk home for lunch simply because he had been let out of school 15 minutes early that day. Normally, he only walked from Lowell Elementary School, located at North 12th Street and Yakima Avenue in Tacoma, Washington, to the nearby Annie Wright Seminary at 827 North Tacoma Avenue, where his sister, Anne, went to school. The two of them usually met the family chauffeur there and were driven home for lunch. But being 15 minutes early, George had decided that he'd rather just walk the extra few blocks home to 420 North Fourth Street. It was about the same distance he would have gone between the schools, and he'd be home before Anne was even let out. At least, that was the plan…and it had seemed pretty logical to him as he cut through the tennis club toward North Borough Road.

But when he reached Borough Road, George came across two men who were parked on the other side of the street in a green 1927 Buick sedan. Dainard, sitting in the passenger seat, couldn't believe his eyes and jumped out of the car, calling to George, "We're a bit lost, kid. I was wondering if you could give us directions on how to get to Stadium Way?"

George squinted at the man who approached him. He looked to be about 40, George thought, with brown hair and a mustache. Who could possibly be on Borough Road, he wondered, without knowing how to get to Stadium Way, seeing as the two roads joined together just a few blocks up? But George was raised to be a polite boy and didn't say any of this. "Sure," he answered, pointing in the direction that the car was already headed. "You just continue up this way…."

George wasn't able to finish his sentence because Dainard suddenly grabbed him, picked him up and carried him across the street to the car. There he threw him in the trunk and covered him in a blanket. "Drive, Harry!"

Dainard hissed to his companion, 24-year-old Harmon Metz Waley, who was in the driver's seat.

"Where are we going?" Waley asked, confused.

"I'll figure it out once you start driving," Dainard replied in a whisper. "The important thing is we got our meal ticket...now we just gotta cash it in." For the next hour, they talked in hushed tones as they drove so George wouldn't be able to hear what they were saying.

Dainard and Waley had met five years earlier in the Idaho State Penitentiary in Boise, where Waley had been serving six months for vagrancy, and Dainard—who often went by the name William Mahan—was serving 20 years for bank robbery. However, Dainard never finished his sentence because, for some unknown reason, he was granted a full pardon on June 1, 1933, by Idaho Governor Charles Ben Ross.

Meanwhile, Waley had headed to Salt Lake City, Utah, shortly after his release, and after a weeklong courtship, married young Margaret Eldora Thulin on November 13, 1933. The couple drifted between Utah, New Jersey and Tacoma, Washington, living off welfare as Waley honed his burglary and robbery skills. In April 1935, Waley ran into Dainard in Salt Lake City, and they all decided to move to Spokane, Washington, together.

On April 13, the three of them rented a house at 1509 11th Avenue in Spokane. On the morning of May 17, 19-year-old Thulin was reading the obituaries in the paper and saw that John Philip Weyerhaeuser Sr.—George's grandfather—had just passed away. The article detailed the large fortune that the family had. Thulin's eyes danced as she thought about all that money.

"Hey, the snatch racket's in vogue these days," she said to the two men, thinking about the kidnapping of famous aviator Charles Lindbergh's 20-month-old son three years earlier and the subsequent rash of similar crimes that had taken place thereafter. Lindbergh's toddler had later been found murdered, but Thulin continued, "We wouldn't have to hurt anyone, and it would be an easy payday."

Perhaps all three of them were genuinely convinced that, if they actually pulled it off, nobody would be hurt. Maybe they didn't think about how such an experience could impact the kidnap victim for life, especially if he was a child when it happened. But one thing's for sure—all of them were highly motivated by the potential money.

The trio drove to Tacoma and rented an apartment in the Fir Apartments at 1402 East Fir Street, across town from the Weyerhaeuser's. From there, Dainard and Waley got to know the family's daily routine, keeping an eye on them for several days and trying to figure out if it would even be possible to kidnap one of them. The children were very rarely on their own without a chauffeur or some other chaperone, making the prospect seem pretty challenging—until George walked right into their waiting arms.

And here they were, driving around with one of the most valuable kids in the world.

Finally, they reached their first destination and stopped at the side of a country road. Dainard opened the trunk and pulled the blanket off George. "Hi, kid," he said. "Nobody's gonna hurt you, but I need you to do one thing.

Take this pencil and write your name on the back of this envelope, okay?"

George dutifully drew out the letters of his name in his best handwriting.

"Thanks, kid," Dainard said, pulling George from the car and tying a blindfold around his head. Then Dainard picked the boy up and carried him across a stream that ran beside the road before putting him back down, as Waley followed.

"We're gonna walk from here," Dainard said, taking George's hand and leading him over rough terrain through the woods for half a mile. Every few steps, a tree branch would brush against George, and he kept losing his balance on the uneven ground, but the three of them continued on. Eventually they came to a large log, and Dainard took off George's blindfold. The boy noticed that a hole had been dug in the ground, about four feet square.

"Get comfy, kid. This is your home for the next little bit," Dainard said, picking George up and placing him in the hole. Waley took George's leg and Dainard took his wrist and together they locked him down with a chain, and then covered the hole with a board. For the next several hours—until 10:00 PM that night—Dainard and Waley took turns standing guard.

Meanwhile, they took the envelope that George had signed and sent a ransom letter to his house, demanding $200,000 in small, unmarked bills in exchange for the boy's safe return. His family had already notified the police, who had been searching for George for hours, when a postal carrier arrived with the special delivery letter at 6:25 PM, addressed "To Whom it May Concern."

"Oh, my goodness, that's George's handwriting!" his mother cried when she saw the back of the envelope.

John Weyerhaeuser Jr. sat down with the typewritten letter, which was signed "Egoist," and went over the 21 points that it laid out. The twelfth point said, "In five days or as soon as you have the money, advertise in the *Seattle Post-Intelligencer* personal column. Say 'We are ready.' And sign it 'Percy Minnie.'" It went on to promise that once that happened, the family would be notified of how to deliver the ransom.

"Hey, Bill, the police must be doing a pretty extensive search of the area…what if they find this hole?" Waley asked when he and Dainard were finally together again later that night.

"Good point," Dainard agreed. "Let's move on."

They removed the cover from George's hole, unchained him, carried him back to the car and locked him in the trunk. Barely making a peep, the boy was driven around for another hour. Then he was taken out and led through the woods again.

"Wait by this tree," Dainard instructed him, as the two men dug another hole, similar to the first. Waley placed a seat from the car into the hole, along with two blankets, while Dainard picked George up and put him in. Then they covered the hole with tar paper.

George gasped as a lizard ran across his leg. He closed his eyes and repeated to himself, "Don't make a sound, and you won't get hurt. Everything's going to be fine."

By the morning, Weyerhaeuser had placed two ads in the Personals column of the *Seattle Post-Intelligencer* Classified Want Ads. The first one read, "Expect to be ready to come

Monday. Answer. Percy Minnie." That was followed by another ad: "Due to publicity beyond our control, please indicate another method of reaching you. Hurry, relieve anguished mother. Percy Minnie."

The next day, on Sunday, May 26, the men took Thulin to the site where George was being kept. The three of them put George in the trunk of a Ford car and drove all the way across Washington into Idaho. They went through Blanchard and continued along the highway to the mountains. In the early morning hours, they took George from the car, handcuffed him to a tree and guarded him until nightfall. Then they took him to a house and made him a makeshift bedroom by putting a mattress, a small white table and two chairs in a big closet.

The FBI had been advised of the kidnapping as soon as the ransom note arrived via the postal service because of the statute that said that sending extortion threats by mail was a felony. Now they had two reasons to get involved, both of them related to the very kidnapping case that had inspired Dainard and the Waleys in the first place. On June 17, 1932, the Federal Kidnapping Act, otherwise known as the Lindbergh Law, had been passed, which also made it a federal felony to take a kidnap victim across a state line. Authorities may not have known for sure that George had been taken out of state, but they suspected as much. Because of that, over a dozen FBI agents were sent to Tacoma to investigate leads in the Weyerhaeuser case.

George was in his closet room on Tuesday, May 28—a day before the kidnapper's original deadline of five days—when Weyerhaeuser put another classified ad in the *Seattle Post-Intelligencer*. It said simply, "We are ready. Percy

Minnie." The press didn't get any further information about the ransom negotiations because the family wanted to keep it a secret, and law enforcement authorities agreed not to interfere with the process until George had been safely released.

The next day, Wednesday, May 29, Weyerhaeuser got a letter from the kidnappers that told him to register at the Ambassador Hotel at 806 Union Street in Seattle at 7:00 PM that very evening and to use the name James Paul Jones. He was promised further instructions once he did so, and inside the envelope was a handwritten note from George saying that he was safe, so Mr. Weyerhaeuser complied with their demands.

At 9:45 PM, the next letter was delivered to him at the hotel by a taxi driver. That letter told him to take the money to the corner of South Renton Avenue and 62nd Avenue South in the Rainier Valley and to look along the right-hand side of the road for a stake with a white cloth attached to it. When he reached the stake, Weyerhaeuser found a tin can under the cloth and a note in the can instructing him to drive another 700 feet straight ahead to a second white cloth, where he was to park with the engine and parking lights on. He did that, but nothing happened for the next three hours, so he went back to the hotel in Seattle.

The next morning at 11:30 AM, he got an anonymous phone call at the hotel, asking why he hadn't followed the instructions in the second note.

"I followed the instructions, but I didn't find a second note," Weyerhaeuser explained.

"You'll be contacted with new instructions, and this will be your last chance to save your son," the voice told him before hanging up.

Weyerhaeuser waited for the instructions all day until finally, at 9:00 PM, he got another phone call from a man speaking in a fake European accent.

"Drive with the money to 1105 East Madison Street and look for a tin can," the man instructed. "It will be directly inside the gate on the right-hand side, and in the can, you'll find a note with further instructions."

That next note told Weyerhaeuser to drive to the Half Way House on the Pacific Highway near Angle Lake, and then turn onto a side road and look for the next note. This led him through a series of notes in tin cans, all marked with makeshift white flags. The final one said he was to park his car with the engine running, interior light on and driver's side door open, leave the bag with the money on the front seat and walk back down the road towards the highway. The note promised that if he had indeed left the $200,000 ransom as instructed, George would be let go within 30 hours.

Weyerhaeuser got about 100 yards down the road before he heard noises behind him. He turned to see someone run from the bushes, jump into his black 1933 Pontiac sedan and drive off. He continued walking to the highway, where he hitched a ride back to Tacoma to wait for word of what would happen next.

The next evening, Friday, May 31, at about 6:00 PM, Dainard told George, "I'll bet you'd like to sleep in your own bed again, instead of in this closet. Don't worry, we'll be leaving here soon, and you'll be going home." Because of that, George didn't try to run away when Dainard and Waley went upstairs, leaving him all alone.

They loaded George into the trunk of the car again and drove back across the border to the Issaquah-Hobart Road, about four miles south of Issaquah, Washington. Around 3:30 AM, the kidnappers left George there, by himself, in the rain.

"Hey kid, just wait here, and your father will come by to take you home," Dainard told him.

"You can stay dry in that little house there," Waley said, pointing to a small decrepit shack set back from the road a bit.

"Here ya go, this will keep you warm," Dainard added, tossing the two dirty blankets from the second dirt hole at George. "You're a good kid, you know that?" he continued, as he stuffed a dollar bill into George's shirt pocket.

"Thanks," George mumbled, looking at the ground and kicking the dirty blankets lying by his feet.

After the kidnappers drove away, George waited a bit for his dad, but then decided to start walking—the second time in just over a week that he had made that decision. This time, however, the consequences weren't as dire. Six miles down the road, he wandered onto Louis P. Bonifas's farm and up to the house.

"I'm George Hunt Weyerhaeuser," he announced to the startled couple inside.

"Oh, my goodness, you poor dear!" exclaimed Mrs. Willena Bonifas, Louis's wife. "Come in, come in, let me get you some breakfast! You must be starving!"

"Yes, ma'am," agreed George, digging into the plate of eggs like he hadn't eaten in a week—which was almost true.

After breakfast, Mrs. Bonifas cleaned George up and gave him a dry pair of socks and shoes to wear.

"Okay, now let's get you home to Tacoma," Mr. Bonifas said gently, ushering George into his dilapidated old Model T Ford.

At 6:30 AM, Bonifas pulled into a Union 76 gas station in Renton.

"Excuse me, could you please telephone the Weyerhaeuser residence for me? Tell them I'm bringing their boy home?" Bonifas asked the attendant, Ernie Backlund.

A few minutes later, Backlund returned and said, "Sorry, sir, no answer."

"Well, keep trying," said Bonifas. Soon, however, he got tired of waiting and called the Tacoma Police Department instead.

"George Weyerhaeuser is safe," he told them. "I'm driving him to Tacoma."

The two started off again along the Pacific Highway, but were intercepted by a taxi about 18 miles outside of Tacoma.

"Hello, sir!" said a man who got out of the cab.

"Hi there!" Bonifas answered back.

"You've done a great job so far. Thank you! I'll take the boy from here," the man told him, smiling at George and giving him a wink. George grinned back shyly.

"Well, I don't know about that," replied Bonifas, looking the man up and down. He seemed respectable enough, but still….

"Your car doesn't look safe enough to go any farther," the man continued, "and we wouldn't want to put you in any danger. But here's five dollars for your trouble…the city of Tacoma sure appreciates it!"

"Are you a police officer?" Bonifas asked, looking at the five-dollar bill as the man ushered George into the cab. George smiled at Bonifas, reassuring him, as he settled into the back seat.

"Yes, sir! You have a good day, now! Thanks again!" the man called, waving cheerily to Bonifas as his taxi pulled away and headed back towards Tacoma.

But the man who took George in his cab wasn't a policeman, he was a reporter—and not even a news reporter, but a sports writer for the *Seattle Times* who was in Tacoma covering the Weyerhaeuser kidnapping story because it was one of the most sensational crimes in the country and all hands were on deck. Besides the crowd of curious bystanders, the Weyerhaeuser mansion had been constantly surrounded by local and syndicated newspaper reporters, newsreel crews, radio broadcasters and photographers, each hoping for the big scoop. And John H. Dreher was the one who got it.

Dreher had been tipped off about George's release near Issaquah and knew that the boy was being driven home in a Model T Ford. Following his gut instinct, he had caught a cab at the Hotel Winthrop at 773 Broadway and started out towards Renton, running into Bonifas along the way just as he'd hoped. He instructed the cab driver to take back roads to return to Tacoma so they would avoid the police and other members of the media. As they drove, George crouched out of sight on the backseat, and Dreher sat next to him on the floor, conducting an exclusive interview with the boy and scribbling furiously in his notebook.

At around 7:45 AM, the taxi pulled into the Weyerhaeusers' garage, and Dreher banged on the basement garage door until a family friend, Henry Marfield Bolcom, opened it.

He and George went quietly into the house, and then Bolcom, who was acting as the family's spokesman, issued a statement to the press. He said that George had been safely returned and asked that they not publish any more details about his kidnapping so that his life wouldn't be further endangered. But it was too late to stop Dreher, who was already back at the Hotel Winthrop writing his story about "the world's most famous kidnap victim" for the front page of the *Seattle Times* "Extra" editions, which was then picked up for nation-wide syndication by The Associated Press.

Meanwhile, now that George was home, the search for the kidnappers began. The press described it as "the greatest manhunt in the history of the Northwest" as local, state and federal law enforcement officers got involved. FBI agents had already made note of the serial numbers that were on each of the 20,000 bills used as ransom money, and that information had been sent to FBI Headquarters in Washington, DC, where an official 10-page list had been prepared for publication and distribution. They had recently solved other high-profile kidnapping cases with this strategy, including the Lindbergh one, and the list was now sent far and wide to banks, post offices, hotels, railroad depots and other commercial places where money changed hands in large quantities.

Later the same morning, Weyerhaeuser's 1933 black Pontiac sedan—the one he had used to pay the ransom money—was found abandoned in Seattle's Chinatown, at Fifth Avenue South and Weller Street. It was searched for evidence and inside was an empty tin can and the black Gladstone bag that had held the money.

The first $20 ransom bill showed up on a Sunday night, June 2, at the Union Pacific station in Huntington, Oregon. The station agent who took it said that a man had used it to buy a ticket for the 10:10 PM train to Salt Lake City. Two days later, someone else used another $20 ransom bill to pay for a postal money order in Spokane.

By Friday, June 7, about 20 of the bills had been found in the cash drawers of various Salt Lake City stores. Most of them were $10 bills, and several had been spent by a young woman to buy food and other items at a Kress' and a Woolworth's 10-cent store. The FBI had the Salt Lake City Police Department post undercover officers in the cashier's cages of every variety store downtown so they'd be on hand to quickly screen serial numbers.

On Saturday, June 8, a Woolworth's clerk brought a $5 bill to the cashier's cage and told Detective William M. Rogers and Patrolman L.B. Gifford—who were there checking serial numbers—that it had just been given to him to pay for a 20-cent purchase. The officers quickly identified it as one of the ransom bills and arrested the woman who had tried to spend it—none other than Margaret Thulin, claiming to be Mrs. Margaret Von Metz.

They took her to the FBI's Salt Lake City Field Office, where agents searched her purse and found another ransom bill. Thulin told several conflicting stories, but finally admitted she lived at 847 Condus Place in a house she had rented just three days before. Agents staked it out, waiting for her husband to arrive, and a few hours later they had arrested Waley, who had "Metz"—his middle name— tattooed on the back of his hand.

Waley kept saying he knew nothing about the Weyerhaeuser kidnapping, but he had two of the ransom bills in his pocket. The FBI searched the Waleys' house and found a stack of bills in the stove, partly burned, that totaled about $3700 all together. Officers gathered up the ashes and the remains of the money and sent it to the FBI Laboratory in Washington, DC, where the bills were later positively identified as being part of the ransom.

Under repeated questioning and after giving several false statements, Waley finally started to spill the beans. He told the police that he and Dainard had kidnapped George and detailed how it had all unfolded. He continued right up to the point where he and Thulin had arrived in Salt Lake City, and he had purchased a Ford Roadster, registering it under the name Herman Von Metz. He claimed that his wife knew nothing about the actual kidnapping until after it had happened, but that she did help them collect the ransom. Thulin was questioned separately and admitted to her part in the whole escapade. Her story matched Waley's, and they both gave detailed signed confessions to the FBI.

That same night, at about 9:00 PM, Dainard went to Thulin's parent's house in Ogden, Utah, as he had arranged with Waley, to get a suitcase he had left there.

Thulin's grandfather answered the door. "Maggie and Harry were here earlier and picked up their suitcase," he told Dainard. "But when they got back to Salt Lake City, they were arrested."

"My God!" Dainard shouted. "Did they get everything they had?" He ran to his car, a brand-new Ford V8 Tudor sedan, and drove off toward Montana as fast as he could.

The police had already found out from Waley that Dainard would be heading there that night, but they arrived too late to catch him. By this time, Waley didn't care what happened to Dainard because he said they were supposed to have split the money evenly, but Dainard had shorted him by $5000.

The next morning, Sunday, June 9, at 6:40 AM, Dainard was seen in Butte, Montana, by Patrolman James Mooney. The officer happened to have arrested him eight years earlier in 1927 for bank robbery, and he spotted Dainard hanging around a gray 1935 Ford Tudor sedan with Utah plates. He didn't know at the time that Dainard was one of the Weyerhaeuser kidnappers, but as Mooney approached, Dainard took off down an alley, climbed over a fence into a backyard and escaped.

Police Chief Jere Murphy and Patrolman Ed O'Connor searched the abandoned Ford and found a suitcase full of hundreds of bills totaling $15,155 wrapped in oilcloth, along with a list of the ransom notes that had been published in the newspaper. The officers took it all back to headquarters, where they confirmed that the serial numbers on the money matched the ones on the ransom list. Murphy alerted the FBI right away and put out a dragnet for Dainard, but he had already disappeared into the foothills of Idaho and Washington, where he hid out for several weeks before heading to California.

When asked where the rest of their take was, the Waleys said they had buried it under a clump of trees near an anthill in Emigration Canyon, six miles east of Salt Lake City. On Monday morning, June 10, FBI special agents dug up a gunnysack containing $90,790 wrapped in black oilcloth, exactly where the Waleys had said it would be.

On Wednesday, June 12, the Waleys were flown back to Tacoma to face kidnapping charges filed with the U.S. District Court. A week later, the Federal Grand Jury in Tacoma charged them and Dainard with conspiracy, extortion and violating the Federal Kidnapping Act. The press speculated that the Waleys would probably plead guilty to the more tolerant federal charges, since the new kidnapping law in Washington State came with an automatic death penalty unless the jury recommended otherwise—and that speculation turned out to be right.

Waley was arraigned on June 21, 1935, and pleaded guilty to kidnapping and conspiracy before U.S. District Court Judge Edward E. Cushman. Since George Weyerhaeuser hadn't been harmed, the maximum sentence Waley could receive was life imprisonment, but because he confessed, he was given 45 years instead, plus two years for conspiracy, to be served concurrently. He went immediately to the McNeil Island Federal Penitentiary, but was transferred to the brand-new Alcatraz Island Federal Penitentiary in San Francisco on July 17. Alcatraz had been established the year before as a maximum-security facility for violent and hopeless criminals.

Thulin was arraigned with her husband and also wanted to plead guilty, but her court-appointed attorney, Stephen J. O'Brien, said it wasn't a good idea because there was nothing in the indictment that could convict her. The next day, Judge Cushman said she should stand trial, entered her plea as "not guilty" and appointed her a trial lawyer— John Francis Dore, the former mayor of Seattle.

On Tuesday, July 9, Thulin went to trial before Cushman in Tacoma. It was over in five days, but included testimony from more than 40 prosecution witnesses. The jury heard about George's trials and tribulations—being locked in a trunk, holed up in the ground, chained to a tree and imprisoned in a closet—and how Thulin had been involved in taking him into Idaho—the key violation of the Federal Kidnapping Act.

Dore only called one defense witness and that was Thulin herself, who testified that she had only found out about the kidnapping the day after it happened, and she went along with the scheme for two reasons: because she had been raised Mormon and had been taught that she must absolutely obey her husband, and because Dainard had threatened to kill both the Waleys and the boy if she didn't help.

"The only reason I tried to plead guilty to the federal kidnapping charges is because the maximum sentence is life imprisonment, and the FBI warned me that death was the automatic penalty for kidnapping in Washington State. I did not intend to let them hang Harmon or myself," she testified near the end of her trial.

It was all over on Saturday morning, July 13, and Judge Cushman explained to the jury that religious beliefs were not a valid excuse for committing a crime but threat of bodily harm might be. After deliberating for close to six hours, the jury found Thulin guilty of both charges.

On Wednesday, July 17, Judge Cushman sentenced Thulin to 20 years in prison for each of the charges of kidnapping and conspiracy, to be served concurrently at the Federal Detention Farm in Milan, Michigan. On her way to prison, she told the press she would not wait for her husband. "If it hadn't been for him, I would not be where I am today," she said. "I'm through with men forever." Of course, she conveniently forgot to mention at any point that the whole thing had been partly her idea in the first place, even if it had been just a passing thought.

But the key player in the caper, William Dainard, was still at large.

In early 1936, bills with altered serial numbers started showing up in stores on the West Coast, and the FBI lab confirmed that they were indeed from the Weyerhaeuser ransom money. Banks and businesses were put on alert to watch out for more.

On February 15, 1936, a man tried to change $300 worth of the bills at the Canadian National Bank of Commerce in Seattle—but it wasn't Dainard. The man with the bushy red hair took off when the teller went to check the money, but he was later identified as 30-year-old Edward Fliss, also known as Frank "Red" Lane, an associate of Dainard's who had spent time in the Idaho State Penitentiary for kidnapping Willaim Barker Kinne, the Idaho lieutenant-governor, in 1929. Now that the FBI had new leads, they increased their efforts to find Dainard.

On Wednesday, May 26, a man exchanged altered bills at two San Francisco banks, and employees at both of them recorded his license plate number as he drove away. The 1935 Ford sedan was registered to Bert E. Cole, a resident of the Ventura Hotel, which was right across the street from the Federal Building. The next morning, two FBI agents found the car, disabled it and set up surveillance on it.

At noon, Dainard got into the vehicle wearing horn-rimmed glasses as a disguise. When the car wouldn't start, he got out to check under the hood, and FBI agents arrested him. He had a semi-automatic pistol on him, as well as $7300 in ransom bills, but didn't resist arrest. Another $30,074 of the money was found hidden in his hotel room.

After being questioned for four hours, Dainard was flown to Tacoma. He wouldn't sign a confession, but he admitted that he had kidnapped George Weyerhaeuser and told the FBI where to find another $14,000 that he had stashed in Utah. In his Los Angeles home, they also found the dyes and paraphernalia he had used to alter the serial numbers on the currency.

On Saturday, May 9, 1936—almost a year after the kidnapping took place—Dainard was arraigned in Tacoma's U.S. District Court before Judge Cushman, just as his cohorts had been. Instead of taking a court-appointed attorney, he pleaded guilty to the charges of kidnapping and conspiracy to kidnap. Because he was recognized as the mastermind behind the kidnapping, he got a much longer sentence—60 years in prison on each count, to be served concurrently. He started serving his sentence immediately at the McNeil Island Federal Penitentiary but was soon transferred to the Federal Penitentiary in Leavenworth, Kansas.

While in prison, they discovered the reason why Dainard had been so willing to lead the kidnapping escapade and to put a child's well-being in danger—Dainard was found to be insane and was committed for a while to a mental hospital in Springfield, Missouri. But then they must have decided that he was sane enough to be kept with other convicts after all, so he was sent to Alcatraz to finish his sentence.

On October 23, 1936, Edward Fliss was arrested by the FBI in San Francisco and readily admitted that Dainard had paid him a 15-percent commission to help launder the ransom money up and down the West Coast, exchanging larger, more traceable bills for smaller denominations. He was charged in Tacoma for conspiracy and being an accessory after the fact to kidnapping; he pleaded guilty to the latter charge, but not guilty to the former, since he had been in jail in Montana when the kidnapping had occurred. After admitting to his previous kidnapping escapade, which he said was "not a real kidnapping" because he let the lieutenant-governor go when he found out who he was, Judge Cushman gave him the maximum penalty—a fine of $5000 and a sentence of 10 years imprisonment at the McNeil Island Federal Penitentiary.

The Weyerhaeuser case was finally closed, and the $157,000 that the FBI had been able to recover was returned to the family.

As a gesture of gratitude for helping George in his hour of need, John Weyerhaeuser Jr. gave Louis Bonifas lifetime employment at the Weyerhaeuser Timber Company's Snoqualmie Falls Lumber Mill and a large monetary reward that allowed Bonifas to buy several acres of land and build a new house near Snoqualmie.

Interestingly, it seems that Weyerhaeuser was not only good at expressing his appreciation, but at forgiving, too. Bonifas wasn't the only figure in the case who was given employment with Weyerhaeuser's company. Waley had written to Weyerhaeuser and apologized several times while serving 28 years of his 45-year sentence and asked if he could have a job when he got out. The family actually gave him that job—at one of the Weyerhaeuser plants in Oregon—upon his release in 1963.

Waley was now a single man; Thulin had divorced him as soon as she got out of prison in 1948. He was also soon working under his former victim, because after graduating from Yale University, George Hunt Weyerhaeuser took over control of the timber company in 1966. Under George's direction as chairman of the board, the Weyerhaeuser Corporation bought out several new businesses and expanded its operations. He retired from the company in 1999.

Dainard was eligible for parole in 1955, but the Federal Parole Board called him a "three-time loser" who didn't deserve an early release. He was finally paroled in 1976 after serving two-thirds of his sentence, and he died in Montana on September 18, 1992, at the age of 90.

CHAPTER TWELVE

Mary Kay Letourneau
The Cradle-Robbing Teacher
(1962–)

When women love us, they forgive us everything, even
our crimes; when they do not love us, they give us credit
for nothing, not even our virtues.

—Honoré de Balzac (1799–1850), French novelist and
playwright

"Vili, wait!" she shouted out of the open window of her minivan, slowing the vehicle down as she pulled up beside him and then rolled to a stop. The 12-year-old boy stopped walking along Washington's Des Moines Marina and got in beside her.

Mary Kay Letourneau looked at young Vili Fualaau gently. "I'm sorry my husband's so rude," she told him. "You didn't need to take off like that. I told you it was okay for you to hang around my house and work on your art projects with my kids. He just doesn't understand."

She tried to brush back the tear that was forming in her eye, but it was no use. Suddenly she was crying.

Fualaau wanted to comfort his former teacher. He had felt close to her for a long time, and it didn't feel like there was a 21-year age difference between them. He had often fantasized about her and had even bet a friend $20 that he could get her to sleep with him. He wanted to grow up, and he wanted to fill a void in his life that he experienced at home. Letourneau had all the pieces of the puzzle.

He reached out and held the 34-year-old woman in his arms, comforting her as she sobbed. He wondered if he dare go further, but figured he had nothing to lose. He leaned over and kissed her, and was pleasantly surprised when she kissed him back. It was like a dam that had long been holding back a torrent of water—or in this case, a flood of passion—had just broken loose, and suddenly they were all over each other, kissing and touching intimately. They moved into the back of the minivan and covered themselves up with a sleeping bag.

Suddenly, they heard a siren and saw flashing lights behind them. A night watchman had called the police, not wanting to approach the suspicious minivan alone.

One of the officers walked up to the car and tapped on the driver's side window. "What's going on here?" he asked.

Scrambling into the front seat, Letourneau rolled the window down. "I'm Mary Kay Letourneau, a schoolteacher," she explained. "I'm watching one of my students overnight because his mother is working a late shift."

"How old is the boy?" the policeman asked.

"Eighteen," she answered.

The officer was puzzled—the kid sure didn't look 18. Had this woman been taken captive by the young boy, dressed in baggy, gangster-style clothes? Or was he the one being held against his will?

"Do you have a driver's license?" he asked the boy.

"No," Fualaau answered.

"State ID card?"

"No, sir."

"How old are you?" the officer persisted.

"Fourteen," answered Fualaau.

At the station, police officers called Vili's mother, Soona Fualaau, at the bakery where she was working the night shift. "Oh, it's okay," she told them. "I trust Mrs. Letourneau. Let her take my son home."

It was June 19, 1996, just five days before Fualaau's 13th birthday. Before he even reached that milestone—becoming a teenager—he would have sexual intercourse with Letourneau for the first time, while her husband was at work and her four children were asleep. By September, when Fualaau started seventh grade at the Highline School District's Cascade Middle School, Letourneau was pregnant with his child.

The pair was about to be caught up in a widely publicized scandal that would make jaws drop, heads shake and fingers wag throughout the nation. A woman formerly regarded as an "all-American girl" was about to have her reputation soiled and tarnished beyond repair. Was it simply poor judgment or a repeating pattern from Letourneau's family history, or was it really a Romeo and Juliet story founded in true love? Nobody but the key players can say how deep the emotions ran, but it might just have been a combination of all three.

Mary Kay Letourneau was born Mary Katherine Schmitz on January 30, 1962, to college professor John and homemaker Mary. Theirs was a devout Roman Catholic family, and Mary Kay—often called "Cake" by her father—was their fourth child and first daughter. They lived in the community of Tustin in Orange County, California.

John began his political career when Mary Kay was two, running for a seat in the state legislature. When he won, the family moved to Sacramento and then kept growing: sister Terry was born in 1965, then Elizabeth and finally Philip.

In 1970, John won a seat in the U.S. House of Representatives, so the family picked up and moved to Washington, DC. As a child, Mary Kay spent a lot of time in Congress, where everyone loved her bubbly personality and well-behaved demeanor. Meanwhile, her mother was getting more involved in conservative political causes, too, campaigning against the Equal Rights Amendment and becoming known as the "West Coast Phyllis Schlafly," referring to another anti-feminist political activist.

In 1972, John was named the presidential candidate for the right-wing American Independent Party, and even though he didn't win, he still received about a million votes. After he lost the race, the family moved back to California to live in Corona del Mar.

On August 11, 1973, the large Schmitz family tragically lost its youngest member. During an informal gathering with friends and family in the backyard, 11-year-old Mary Kay was supposed to be watching her three-year-old baby brother, Philip. Suddenly realizing that she didn't know where he was, she alerted the family, and they all started searching for him. When they found him at the bottom of the pool, he had already drowned.

"I only left him for a minute…just a minute," Mary Kay kept repeating. Later she would say that it had been an accident and nobody was to blame, but she reportedly felt that her parents always blamed her. Either way, it must have been devastating for her.

Mary Kay's teenage years were full of partying, boys, traveling and cheerleading at her Roman Catholic high school. Oddly for a future schoolteacher, she put little importance on her schoolwork and her grades weren't that good.

Her mother expanded her conservative political exploits by becoming a debater on a political commentary TV show called *Free For All*. She presented herself as well-groomed and articulate, espousing many of the same views as her husband, but all the things they had in common didn't stop him from straying.

Ironically, one of the viewpoints they shared—and the one that Mary Schmitz made a plea for on television—was traditional family values and the importance of marriage. But while Mary was arguing for their moral beliefs in public, a sex scandal involving her husband's private life was about to break.

John had been having a long-term affair with one of his former college students, Carla Stuckle, and had fathered two children with her. The scandal became public knowledge after Stuckle was accused of neglecting their first child, John George, when he was a baby. Apparently, John George's penis had been injured by a hair that had been left tightly wrapped around it for a long time, and he needed to have surgery. The operation was a success, but 43-year-old Stuckle wasn't allowed to take her son home because it looked as though the hair had been deliberately tied there, in a square knot, rather than caught accidentally.

Child-abuse investigators went to her home, where the frazzled woman was also caring for baby daughter Eugenie, who was her second child with Schmitz. When Stuckle refused to give the babies' father's name, a detective told her she'd be going to jail and would never see her son again unless she came clean.

"Well, it's John Schmitz…the state senator," she finally revealed. The officers didn't believe that the politician who preached family values could possibly have fathered this woman's children, but after they quietly took him aside and asked him about Stuckle at a meeting of the John Birch Society, Schmitz admitted that the boy was his.

"But I don't support him financially," he told them. "He's her responsibility." When asked about the hair on the child's penis, he said he knew nothing about it.

Like his daughter Mary Kay would in the future, John Schmitz made headlines across the nation for having out-of-wedlock children with his former student. The scandal ended his political career as well as his wife's TV career and put a lot of strain on the family, but unlike his daughter, it didn't end his marriage. John and Mary Schmitz separated for a while, but then got back together.

The hair wasn't enough evidence to charge Stuckle with child abuse, so John George was given back to her. In 1994, she died of complications from diabetes, but since John Schmitz wouldn't take custody of the children—who were now 13 and 11—famous psychic Jeanne Dixon, who was a good friend of Mary Schmitz, did instead. It only lasted a few years though, because Dixon died in 1997 and the illegitimate Schmitz kids were sent to an orphanage.

Through all of this, Mary Kay stood by her father, saying that her mother was a cold and unaffectionate person who "drove him to it." She may have felt the same way about her own husband, Steve.

In college, Mary Kay was attractive and had no problems getting dates. When she met Steve Letourneau, they were instantly attracted to each other and had a lot of fun together, but she never pictured herself spending the rest of her life with him.

In 1984, Mary Kay found out she was pregnant. Like her parents, she was totally against abortion but wrestled with the choice between marrying Steve or raising the baby on her own. One day in the middle of class, she suffered a miscarriage; however, it turned out she was carrying twins, and the second embryo survived to full term.

Meanwhile, at her parents' urging, she married Steve on June 30, 1984, just a few months before their first child, Steve Jr., was born. She wasn't in love and didn't think her husband was very smart or mature, but she did like spending time with him. How odd that she would later fall for a much younger guy but feel that he was mature enough.

That younger guy had just celebrated his first birthday: little Vili Fualaau, a Samoan-American boy, was born on June 24, 1983, to Luaiva and Soona Fualaau. Vili's father, Luaiva, was sometimes a preacher, sometimes an auto mechanic, but more often a prison inmate who barely knew his son...not to mention the 17 other children he had sired with a total of five different women.

After getting married, the Letourneaus dropped out of college and moved to Steve's hometown of Anchorage, Alaska, where he found work as a baggage handler for Alaska Airlines. But from the beginning, the marriage was in trouble. First, there were the constant financial issues, which caused Mary Kay to beg her parents for money, and then there were all the extramarital affairs that Steve kept having.

A year later they moved to Seattle, where Steve had been transferred, and the family started to grow. In 1987, Mary Claire was born, followed by Nicholas in 1991 and Jacqueline in 1993—a total of two boys and two girls.

Mary Kay found that she had a gift for working with children and decided she wanted to become a teacher, so she took courses at Seattle University in the evenings after caring for the kids all day. In 1989, she graduated and got a job that fall as a second grade teacher at the Shorewood Elementary School in the Seattle suburb of Burien.

The kids loved this attractive, energetic teacher, and everyone wanted to be in her class. Mary Kay was good at nurturing and motivating them, and had a habit of offering every student a choice of H.H.H. at the end of the day: a high-five, a handshake or a hug.

The only problems with her classes were her chronic lateness and a bit of chaos, since she didn't like to discipline the kids. The lateness, she claimed, was because Steve would let the kids stay up until she got home, so she couldn't prepare her lesson plans until after she had put them all to bed, making for some pretty late nights.

Mary Kay had always paid special attention to children she thought were gifted, and Vili Fualaau was talented in art. When she found him in her second grade class, she encouraged him quite a lot—maybe more so because the odds were against him. His family lived in a poor area of Des Moines called White Center—also called "Rat City" because it was overrun with rodents. His father was back in prison for armed robbery, and his mother worked long hours in a bakery. Letourneau later said that they bonded almost instantaneously but developed a deeper respect and understanding over time. She bought him art supplies and introduced him to the piano, then continued to mentor him even when he was no longer her pupil.

Letourneau had an eventful year in 1995, some of it good, some of it bad. She had another miscarriage, and then found out that her father had terminal cancer. When she turned to her husband for comfort, Steve showed no compassion. But while her personal life was going downhill, her professional life was looking up; she got a promotion at the school and was assigned to teach fifth and sixth graders.

As the new school year started, a familiar face showed up in her class: Vili Fualaau, now 12 years old. This time around, their relationship deepened even further, and the boy took up more and more of her time and energy. He often stayed late with her in the classroom, and in turn, she regularly invited him over to have dinner or to spend the night at her house. When they were together, she would flirt with him, once going so far as to tell him that she'd remove one piece of clothing for every correct answer on his history test.

He was infatuated, too, and Letourneau would later say she ignored his advances and seduction attempts at first. But Fualaau had no problem attracting girls his age and didn't see why Letourneau should be any different. He gave her gifts to woo her—poems, drawings and one time even a sterling silver ring he had found on the street.

"Will you marry me?" he asked shyly.

"Of course, I will," she answered, slipping off her wedding ring and putting Vili's ring in its place. For the rest of the year, the only time she took Vili's ring off while at school was when her husband came by. Fualaau asked her when he could have a kiss, and she promised him that it would happen on the last day of school.

His classmates labeled him one of the teacher's pets, but by the time the semester was winding down in April 1996, other teachers were becoming increasingly puzzled by their behavior. To them, it didn't seem so much like a teacher with a favorite student, but like two teenagers making eyes at each other.

As the school year ended, the two of them decided to take art classes together at Highline Community College and a Seattle art store, and Mary Kay convinced Steve to let the boy come with them on the family trip to Alaska.

And, of course, as the student-teacher relationship ended between Mary Kay Letourneau and Vili Fualaau, the sexual relationship was just starting: their first kiss in the minivan, their first intercourse days before Fualaau's 13th birthday and Letourneau's subsequent pregnancy with their first child by the end of the summer.

Even though she had known him since he was seven years old, Letourneau saw him as a man, saying, "He dominated me in the most masculine way that any man, any leader, could do. I trusted him and believed in him and in our future." That brings up the question of how emotionally and psychologically mature Letourneau was. And despite the fact that she said Vili was very emotionally mature for his age, it's a lot of pressure to put on a kid…and it was about to increase even more.

While seventh-grader Fualaau was now attending a different school, he'd still drop by daily to see the woman he considered his girlfriend. By October 1996, Letourneau was telling friends that she had found her soulmate and was in love. While she was pregnant, she wanted Steve to think it was his, so she coerced him into having sex more often. She figured that when the mixed-race baby was born, she'd have an excuse to get the divorce she'd been afraid to ask for.

But somewhere along the way he figured it out and confided to relatives that he thought his wife was "pregnant by that 13-year-old" with a "nigger baby." He started shouting at her in front of their kids and hitting her—even going so far as to punch her in the stomach repeatedly to try to cause a miscarriage. Other times, he tried to convince her to terminate the pregnancy, a sentiment that her own mother—the steadfast anti-abortionist—seconded.

In February 1997, Steve found some love letters that his wife had written to Fualaau. He then told his cousin, who made a couple of anonymous phone calls on February 25, first alerting Child Protection Services and then the Highline School District Officials. The report was forwarded to police, and on March 4, Letourneau was pulled out of a teachers' meeting and arrested on charges of second-degree child rape—a more disturbing term for what's commonly called "statutory rape." In the interrogation room, she broke down and cried.

Letourneau remained free on bail while she waited for her baby to be born, but she was left to live alone. To keep them out of the media spotlight, her four other children were sent to Washington, DC, to stay with relatives for a while, without her knowledge. Just like her father had, Mary Kay found her name splashed across news headlines for having sex—and a baby—with a former student…and it tore her family apart the same way. It also impacted her students, who lost their favorite teacher and heard her derogatorily called a "child rapist."

Investigators looked into whether she had ever touched another child inappropriately, including her own, but quickly established that Fualaau had been the only one. He always maintained that he wasn't a victim and hadn't been traumatized, and his mother agreed. Even though she didn't approve of the relationship, she said that the case shouldn't have been prosecuted.

Meanwhile, Mary Kay was ordered to undergo a series of psychiatric examinations. She demonstrated extreme mood swings and was diagnosed with bipolar disorder, formerly called manic-depressive disorder. Dr. Julia Moore felt the condition must have contributed to Mary Kay's careless behavior and prescribed mood-stabilizing drugs and psychotherapy.

On May 23, 1997, Mary Kay and Vili's daughter, Audrey Lokelani Fualaau, was born in Seattle's Swedish Hospital. She was named after an aunt of Mary Kay's, while her middle name means "rose of heaven" in Samoan. Against court orders, Letourneau let Vili spend as much time as he wanted at her house with their newborn, and soon the 14-year-old father was changing diapers and making formula.

Meanwhile, public opinion about the situation was greatly divided. The pair started garnering some sympathy, but people wondered if it was simply because she was a woman, and one with such an innocent and pure image at that. She didn't fit the stereotype of what a sex offender looks or acts like. But if a 35-year-old male teacher had gotten his 13-year-old female student pregnant, wouldn't he already be in jail and likely locked up forever?

While Mary Kay insisted that she didn't deserve to be punished for sexual activity that was motivated by love, her critics said the same excuse from a man would be ridiculed. On the other hand, her supporters said that you can't compare a 13-year-old girl getting pregnant and carrying the child to term to a 13-year-old boy who merely got someone else pregnant. Besides that, they noted that the male has to be aroused in order for intercourse to take place…so it couldn't have happened without the boy's consent.

In fact, both parties agreed that the sex had been initiated by Fualaau, and that he had enjoyed it. But while in some states statutory rape charges only apply if the female is the minor, in Washington, the child rape law is gender neutral, which meant that, no matter what way you sliced it, Mary Kay was a rapist and Vili was her victim.

On August 7, 1997, Letourneau got her day in court. Vili's mother, Soona Fualaau, testified that she had forgiven Letourneau and felt that she'd been punished enough for her mistake. She requested that, rather than jail time, Letourneau be given treatment as a sex offender.

After Letourneau made sure that everyone understood that the relationship was "romantic" and "consensual," she pleaded guilty to two counts of child rape. This was based on a deal her lawyer had worked out for her: she would plead guilty, take her meds for at least six months and go to jail for three. After that, she would take part in the sex offender treatment program.

Superior Court Judge Linda Lau said she'd accept the plea bargain, but only if Mary Kay would give up custody of Audrey to Soona while she was behind bars and never again have contact with Vili. Letourneau agreed to the terms.

On November 14, her sentencing hearing was held before Judge Lau, and over 100 photographers and reporters were there to document it.

"Your honor, I did something that I had no right to do, morally or legally," Mary Kay told Judge Lau before sentencing, sniffling and holding back tears. "It was wrong and I am sorry. I give you my word that it will not happen again. Please help me. Help us all."

Judge Lau sentenced Letourneau to seven and a half years in prison, but suspended all but six months of it and gave her credit for time already served. Lau stated that expert testimony and the wishes of the victim's family made her believe that community-based treatment was the best choice.

"It will not be easy," Lau told Letourneau. "You will not simply be released into the community to resume your former life. From the moment you are released and for the next few years, your life will not be your own."

Mary Kay either didn't understand that or chose to ignore it—as well as the promises she made in court. After serving another 80 days, she was released from jail in January 1998…but only temporarily, as it turned out.

She immediately stopped taking her medication—which some say may have influenced her later decisions—then registered as a sex offender as required and moved in with a friend in the Seward Park neighborhood of Seattle. She had not only lost custody of the four Letourneau kids, who were now living with their father in Alaska, but her house had been sold. Obviously, she also had no job, since as a convicted sex offender, she was banned for life from teaching—at least in all Washington public schools. In fact, until she finished three years of sex offender treatment, she wouldn't be allowed to have unsupervised contact with any minors at all—not even her own children.

But none of that was on Letourneau's mind during those few weeks; instead, she was thinking about Fualaau. At 2:40 AM on February 3, Seattle police officers on a routine neighborhood patrol of Seward Park stopped by a parked car with steamed-up windows, as if someone was having sex inside. After ordering the occupants to open the door, the officers immediately recognized Mary Kay and Vili Fualaau, now a high school freshman. They also found a passport, baby clothes and a box with $6500 cash inside, which seemed to indicate that the couple had been planning to leave town with their nine-month-old baby. Letourneau later claimed that she wasn't planning any such thing—the money was to pay her lawyer and the passport was just for identification.

Either way, Letourneau was arrested for violating parole, and, three days later, she was back in court. More than 125 journalists were there, noting that she looked much more disheveled and flustered than the first time. Letourneau's attorney, David Gehrke, pleaded for leniency, saying, "The only person that really needs to be protected from Mary Kay Letourneau is Mary Kay Letourneau." Letourneau cried silently as he spoke.

But Judge Lau told her it wasn't the system that was flawed; on the contrary, Letourneau had foolishly squandered her opportunity at leniency. The prosecutor and probation officer both said she was a manipulator who didn't feel she had done anything wrong, and therefore, they didn't believe she would benefit from simple treatment. The plea bargain was vacated, and Letourneau got the maximum penalty for child rape: her original sentence of seven and a half years, to be served at the Washington Corrections Center for Women at Gig Harbor.

Letourneau said she actually didn't mind going back to prison, because at least there she was allowed to see her five kids when they came to visit, unlike when she was on probation. And that became an even bigger deal when she found out she was going to have a sixth child.

Back behind bars, prison officials soon discovered that Letourneau was pregnant again with Fualaau's second child but decided not to prosecute her for child rape again. In October 1998, she gave birth to another daughter, named Georgia Alexis Fualaau, in a Tacoma hospital. Like Audrey, Alexis went to live with 15-year-old Vili and his mother, Soona, who legally had custody of both girls.

In February 1999, Fualaau appeared on *The Oprah Winfrey Show* and announced, "I plan to marry her. She's my world, she's my life." In November of that year, Mary Kay was put in solitary confinement for six months because guards intercepted some of the many letters and notes she had been writing to Fualaau. They were packed with the frozen breast milk she was sending to Soona for her new-born daughter, and she had even written on the milk bags in code—104 for "I love you" and other numbers to indicate how she was feeling, or if something was going wrong.

Then the Romeo and Juliet part of the tale was tarnished slightly. First, Fualaau sold some of Mary Kay's love letters to tabloids. Then in 2002, Soona and 18-year-old Vili filed a lawsuit against the Des Moines Police Department and the Highline School District seeking one million dollars in damages for failing to prevent his and Mary Kay's relationship.

"I'm not in love anymore," Vili testified. "I can't see us together in the future. Personally, I've lost feelings for her." He went on to say that the relationship had left him an emotional wreck.

It was unclear whether he had really fallen out of love or was just hoping for a big payday since the Fualaau family was near broke. But he had admitted enough times in public, including then, that he was madly in love, and none of the jury members believed that his feelings had really changed. Fualaau would later admit that they had been right—his lawyer and mother had convinced him that the lawsuit would be a good way to get some money to raise the children. In any case, the defense argued that the relationship had been unforeseeable, and the jury ruled against the Fualaaus.

On Wednesday, August 4, 2004, 42-year-old Mary Kay Letourneau was released from prison after completing her sentence. Once again, the media spotlight tried to shine on her, but she slipped out under cover of darkness. Then she went to the King County Sheriff's Office to register as a level two sex offender—one that's likely to reoffend—something that she would have to do in every county she lived in for the rest of her life, unless ruled otherwise by a judge.

However, one restriction that was removed was the no-contact order between Letourneau and Fualaau, which was rescinded on August 6 by a Seattle judge. Fualaau signed the motion to lift it, saying he wasn't afraid of Letourneau and was now a 21-year-old adult who wanted to see whomever he chose. When he got the call that it was okay to see her again, he broke out in a big grin and felt a tremendous amount of relief.

After that, Romeo and Juliet were on again. People started wondering whether Fualaau had been lying when he had said, two years earlier, that he was no longer in love, or whether he had fallen in love all over again, or whether they were putting on a show for the media—in which case, it's been a really long show.

The latter opinion was the most prevalent among many people at the time. Since Mary Kay had insisted so many times that they were soulmates in love, not a rapist and her victim, the only way to save face and prove herself right would be to resume the relationship upon her release from prison. But, as people started noticing, it wasn't just the same kind of relationship as they had had before; instead, the couple got engaged.

On October 11, 2004, Mary Kay appeared on *Larry King Live* sporting her new engagement ring. She admitted that when she had started having sex with the preteen, she knew it wasn't normal but hadn't realized it was a felony.

"I didn't think about the age, but I thought about running, far and fast," she explained. "I didn't want to be in love at that time in my life."

Shortly after 10:00 PM on Friday, May 20, 2005, 43-year-old Mary Kay and 21-year-old Vili exchanged wedding vows that they had written themselves at the Columbia Winery in Seattle's Woodinville suburb. Only exclusive cameras from *Entertainment Tonight* were allowed inside, but hoards of other media crews were waiting just outside the gates. Vili wore a black tuxedo, and Mary Kay wore a traditional long white wedding gown. Since her father had died of cancer in 2001—while she had been in prison and hadn't been allowed to attend the funeral—her brother, Timmy, stepped in to give her away. Letourneau's teenage daughter Mary Claire was her maid of honor, and a former prison mate was one of the bridesmaids. The couple's two daughters, eight-year-old Audrey and seven-year-old Alexis, were the flower girls.

The couple reportedly earned up to a million dollars by selling the rights to their wedding video footage. That, again, got people wondering about the strength and longevity of the union. Once more, the question arose: Was it true love? Could it even possibly be?

A year later, still together, they appeared on *Dateline NBC* to discuss their life and history, as well as their desire to get full custody of their daughters, to have another baby and for Mary Kay to go back to teaching, perhaps at a community college or private school.

Dateline correspondent Josh Mankiewicz brought up the fact that some people couldn't believe that their relationship was for real, to which Mary Kay replied, "I don't think anyone would listen to this, and really listen to us, and then say that."

Vili added, "If they say that it's not right for us to be together, I don't care. I'm just gonna live my life with her."

While critics still denounce the relationship, saying that it could imply that it's okay for an adult to have sex with a minor as long as they call it love, the Fualaaus appear to have a stable, happy marriage. At the time of writing, they were doing a regular series of events together in Seattle called "Hot for Teacher Night." Mary Kay serves as the official host, while Vili, using the name DJ Headline, spins the dance tracks at Fuel Sports Eats & Beats.

Protesters here and there have accused the events of promoting the raping of children. However, Mike Morris, the club's co-owner, says, "It wouldn't be funny if it was a situation that was happening right now. But it's a situation that happened a long time ago. She served her time. Now they're married; they had kids together. And we're just having fun."

Notes on Sources

Bill Miner

Anderson, Frank W. *Old Bill Miner: Last of the Famous Western Bandits*. British Columbia: Heritage House, 2001.

Foss, Larry. "Outlaw Bill Miner." outlawbillminer.com/main.html.

Gibson, Elizabeth. *Outlaw Tales of Washington: True Stories of Washington's Most Nefarious Crooks, Culprits and Cutthroats*. Guilford, CT: Morris Book Publishing, 2002.

Murphy, Angela. *Canadian Crimes & Capers: A Rogue's Gallery of Notorious Escapades*. Edmonton, AB: Folklore Publishing, 2004.

Veltri, Christopher A. "Billy Miner & Canada's First Train Robbery." www.allthingswilliam.com/willynilly/billy-miner.html.

Yuskavitch, Jim. *Outlaw Tales of Oregon: True Stories of Oregon's Most Infamous Robbers, Rustlers, and Bandits*. Guilford, CT: Morris Book Publishing, 2007.

Sarah Johnson

Associated Press. "Idaho Teen Sentenced to Life Without Chance of Parole." *The Seattle Times*, June 30, 2005. community.seattletimes.nwsource.com/archive/?date=20050630&slug=webidahoteen30.

Friedman, Cassidy. "More Appeals Pending in Johnson Case." *Magic Valley Times-News*, July 5, 2008. www.magicvalley.com/articles/2008/07/05/news/local_state/139827.txt.

Grodd, Elizabeth R., and Jeffrey L. Diamond. "Prime Time Crime: Teen Charged with Parents' Gruesome Murder." *ABC News*. August 13, 2008. abcnews.go.com/print?id= 3451371.

Smith, Terry. "Sarah Johnson Appeals Murder Convictions."*Idaho Mountain Express*, August 9, 2006. www.mtexpress.com/index2.php?ID=2005111713.

Smith, Terry. "New Evidence Surfaces in Johnson Case." *Idaho Mountain Express*, February 27, 2009. www.mtexpress.com/index2.php?ID=2005125027.

Supreme Court of the State of Idaho. *Sarah Marie Johnson, Defendant*. Docket No. 33312. June 26, 2008. www.isc.idaho.gov/opinions/sarahmjohnson.pdf.

Franz Edmund Creffield

Beck, Katherine K. "Seattle Holy Rollers Killings: The Spectacular End to an Oregon Love Cult." HistoryLink.org, December 2, 2003. www.historylink.org/index. cfm?DisplayPage=output.cfm&file_id=4263.

McCracken, T. and Robert B. Blodgett. *Holy Rollers: Murder and Madness in Oregon's Love Cult*. Idaho: Caxton Press, 2002.

Phillips, Jim and Rosemary Gartner. "Murdering Holiness: The Trials of Franz Creffield and George Mitchell." *Journal of Criminal Law and Criminology*, Fall 2004. findarticles.com/ p/articles/mi_hb6700/is_1_95/ai_n29148502/.

Phinney, Mark. "Benton County Churches: Holy Rollers." *WPA Historical Records*, Benton Co., OR. www.rootsweb. ancestry.com/~orbenton/wpa/HolyRoll.html.

Thompson, Lewis. "Nemesis of the Nudist High Priest." *Startling Detective Magazine*, March 1951, Vol. 42, No. 244. www.negativespin.com/joshua2nd.htm.

Keith Hunter Jesperson

"Abducted by a Serial Killer." *The Oprah Winfrey Show*, September, 17, 2009. www.oprah.com/media/20090828-tows-dr-phil-dawn-serial-killer.

Boer, Peter. *Canadian Crime Investigations: Hunting Down Serial Killers*. Edmonton, AB: Folklore Publishing, 2006.

Cook, M. Bridget, and Melissa G. Moore. *Shattered Silence: The Untold Story of a Serial Killer's Daughter*. www.shatteredsilencebook.com.

"Dr. Phil Returns with a Bone-Chilling Story." *The Oprah Winfrey Show*, September 17, 2009. www.oprah.com/article/oprahshow/20090828-tows-dr-phil.

King, Gary C. "Keith Hunter Jesperson." *TruTV Crime Library*. www.trutv.com/library/crime/serial_killers/predators/jesperson/murder_1.html.

Krueger, Peggy, Kendra Justice, and Amy Hunt. *Keith Hunter Jesperson: Happy Face Killer*. Radford, VA: Department of Psychology, Radford University, 2006.

Mari, Will. "Daughter of Serial Killer Confronts Her Past." *Seattle Times*, October 30, 2008. seattletimes.nwsource.com/html/localnews/2008328674_daughterofmurderer30.html.

Moore, Melissa Grace Jesperson. *Melissa Moore: Shattered Silence*. www.melissagracemoore.com.

Olsen, Jack. *I: The Creation of a Serial Killer*. New York, NY: St. Martin's Press, 2002.

Rice, Stephanie. "Daughter of Camas Woman's Killer Seeks Dr. Phil's Help." *The Columbian*, October 27, 2008. columbian.com/article/20081028/NEWS02/710289980.

Sarche, Jon. "America Online Will Remove Serial-Killer Site; Klaas Had Complained." *Seattle Times*, September 12, 1997. community.seattletimes.nwsource.com/archive/?date=19970912&slug=2560066.

Scott, Toni. "Sole Survivor: Telling Her Story After 19 Years." *Chico Enterprise Record*, September 17, 2009. www.chicoer.com/news/.

Clarence Dayton Hillman

"Algona History." City of Algona. www.cityofalgona.com/algonahistory.asp.

De Leon, Joseph M. "Hillman City." *Seattle Times*, September 22, 2007. seattletimes.nwsource.com/html/realestate/2003895938_realneighborhood230.html.

"Jail and Fine for Hillman; Seattle Real Estate Operator Guilty of Fraudulent Use of the Mails." *The New York Times*, April 2, 1911. query.nytimes.com/gst/abstract.html?res=9F04EEDD1431E233A25751C0A9629C946096D6CF.

Jaquette, Leslee. "The Peaceful Pleasures of Boston Harbor." *Sea Magazine*, May 1, 2000. goboatingamerica.com/destinations/DM_article.asp?id=728.

McAbee, J. Clark. "White River Rapscallion: An Insight into C.D. Hillman." *White River Journal*, October 2003. www.wrvmuseum.org/journal/journal_1003.htm.

Wilma, Daved. "Hillman, Clarence Dayton (1870-1935)."
HistoryLink.org, March 10, 2001. www.historylink.org/
index.cfm?DisplayPage=output.cfm&file_id=3080.

Ted Bundy

Bell, Rachael. "Ted Bundy, Notorious Serial Killer." *TruTV Crime Library*. www.trutv.com/library/crime/serial_
killers/notorious/bundy/index_1.html.

Bellamy, Patrick. "Robert D. Keppel, PhD: An Interview."
TruTV Crime Library. www.trutv.com/library/crime/
criminal_mind/profiling/keppel1/1.html.

Lohr, David. "Ted Bundy: The Poster Boy of Serial Killers."
Crime Magazine Encyclopedia of Crime.
www.crimemagazine.com/ted_bundy.htm.

Michaud, Steven G. "The Only Living Witness: The True
Story of Serial Sex Killer Ted Bundy." *TruTV Crime
Library*. www.trutv.com/library/crime/criminal_mind/
psychology/witness/1.html.

Supreme Court of Florida. *Theodore Robert Bundy, Appellant*.
Appeal No. 59,128. December 15, 1982.
www.law.fsu.edu/library/flsupct/59128/59128ini.pdf.

Maxwell Levy

Gibson, Elizabeth. "Levy, Maxwell (d. 1931), Port Townsend's
Crimper King." HistoryLink.org, December 5, 2006.
www.historylink.org/index.cfm?DisplayPage=output.
cfm&file_id=7763.

Linda Burfield Hazzard

Beck, Katherine. "Hazzard, Linda Burfield (1867–1938): Fasting Proponent and Killer." HistoryLink.org, October 26, 2006. www.historylink.org/index.cfm?DisplayPage= output.cfm&file_id=7955.

Hazzard, Linda Burfield. *Fasting and the Cure of Disease*. Seattle, WA: Harrison Publishing, 1908.

Olsen, Gregg. *Starvation Heights: A True Story of Murder and Malice in the Woods of the Pacific Northwest*. New York, NY: Three Rivers, 1997.

Olsen, Gregg. *Starvation Heights*. Official website. www.starvationheights.com.

Ramsland, Katherine. "Angels of Death: The Doctors." *TruTV Crime Library*. www.trutv.com/library/crime/serial_killers/weird/doctors/11.html.

Robert Stevenson

King, Gary C. "Dragnet for Portland's Sex Crazed Monster." *Investigation Discovery Classic True Crime Stories*. investigation.discovery.com/investigation/true-crime-stories/robert-stevenson/robert-stevenson.html.

Oregon Department of Corrections. *Oregon Offender Search*. docpub.state.or.us/OOS/intro.jsf.

Oregon Department of Corrections. *Snake River Correctional Institution*. www.oregon.gov/DOC/PUBAFF/docs/pdf/ IB_67_SRCIfacts.pdf.

Gary Ridgway

Bell, Rachael. "Green River Killer: River of Death." *TruTV Crime Library*. www.trutv.com/library/crime/serial_killers/predators/greenriver/index_1.html.

Staff of the King County Journal. *Gary Ridgway: The Green River Killer*. Seattle, WA: King County Journal, 2003.

Wilma, David. "Gary Leon Ridgway Pleads Guilty to Murdering 48 Green River Killer Victims on November 5, 2003." HistoryLink.org, November 5, 2003. www.historylink.org/index.cfm?DisplayPage=output.cfm&file_id=4262.

William Dainard

"Famous Cases: The Weyerhaeuser Kidnapping." FBI History. www.fbi.gov/libref/historic/famcases/weyer/weyer.htm.

Glass, Andrew. "This Day on Capitol Hill: February 13." *The Politico*, February 12, 2007. www.politico.com/news/stories/0207/2725.html.

McClary, Daryl C. "Weyerhaeuser Kidnapping." HistoryLink.org, March 27, 2006. www.historylink.org/index.cfm?DisplayPage=output.cfm&file_id=7711.

McClary, Daryl C. "FBI Arrest William Dainard, Mastermind of the Weyerhaeuser Kidnapping, in San Francisco on May 7, 1936." HistoryLink.org, May 4, 2006. www.historylink.org/index.cfm?DisplayPage=output.cfm&file_id=7749.

Wanted Broadside: Weyerhaeuser Kidnapping, Dainard, William. Antiquarian Booksellers' Association of America. www.abaa.org/books/201046740.html.

Mary Kay Letourneau

Associated Press. "Letourneau Marries Fualaau Amid Media Circus." *Seattle Post-Intelligencer*, May 21, 2005. www.seattlepi.com/local/225292_wedding21.html.

Fualaau, Vili. DJ Headline MySpace page. www.myspace.com/djheadline.

Goldsmith, Samuel. "Mary Kay Hosts 'Hot for Teacher' with Victim-Turned-Husband Vili Fualaau as DJ." *New York Daily New*s. www.nydailynews.com/gossip/2009/05/24/2009-05-24_mary_kay_letourneau_hosts_hot_for_teacher_with_victimturnedhusband_vili_fualaau_.html.

Ho, Vanessa and Sam Skolnik. "Letourneau Registers as Sex Offender." *Seattle Post-Intelligencer*. www.seattlepi.com/local/184960_order05.html.

Mankiewicz, Josh. "A Love Like No Other." *Dateline NBC*, June 2, 2006. www.msnbc.msn.com/id/13106958//%20 interviews.

Noe, Denise. "Mary Kay Letourneau: The Romance That Was a Crime." *TruTV Crime Library*. www.trutv.com/library/crime/criminal_mind/psychology/marykay_letourneau/1.html.

Purse, Marcia. *Mary Kay Letourneau: Criminal – Or Victim of Bipolar Disorder?* About.com: Bipolar Disorder, November 29, 2006. bipolar.about.com/cs/crime/a/0001_marykay.htm.

Stritof, Sheri and Bob Stritof. "Mary Kay Letourneau Marriages." About.com: Marriage. marriage.about.com/od/celebritymarriages/a/letourneau.htm.

Tate, Cassandra. "Letourneau, Mary Kay (b. 1962)." HistoryLink.org, August 5, 2004. www.historylink.org/index.cfm?DisplayPage=output.cfm&file_id=5727.

Heather Vale Goss

Heather Vale Goss became fascinated with the study of human behavior at a very young age. Instrumental in the launch of one of the first multimedia current affairs websites, she also worked as a traffic reporter, a news anchor and an online radio talk-show host. She currently calls Oregon home, where she runs an online publishing company with her husband. She investigates the human mind through her studies and publications, and feels that the mindset to achieve greatness and the mindset to commit crimes can be completely opposite, but very much related at the same time.